KU-014-949

INSTITUTE OF ECONOMICS &
STATISTICS LIBRARY OXFORD

1 JUN 1988

RA 412

G 7
· GRE

EVERYONE A PRIVATE PATIENT

EVERYONE
A PRIVATE PATIENT
An Analysis of the Structural Flaws in the
NHS and How They Could be Remedied

David G. Green

IEA

Institute of Economic Affairs
1988

First published in May 1988
by
THE INSTITUTE OF ECONOMIC AFFAIRS
2 Lord North Street, Westminster, London SW1P 3LB

© The Institute of Economic Affairs 1988

Hobart Paperback 27

All rights reserved

ISSN 0309-1783
ISBN 0-255 36210-2

Printed in Great Britain by
Goron Pro-Print Co. Ltd., Lancing, W. Sussex

Filmset in Times Roman 11 on 12 point

CONTENTS

Contents

'An economist is someone who tries to prove that what works in practice also works in theory, except in health care. Some health economists seek to prove that what works in practice cannot work in theory.'

Professor ALAIN ENTHOVEN

FOREWORD

Dr Cento Veljanovski

Research & Editorial Director
Institute of Economic Affairs

THE WELFARE state has been a perennial concern of the Institute of Economic Affairs. For thirty years IEA authors have analysed, criticised and put forward alternative proposals. The hallmarks of these efforts have been their emphasis on choice, competition and individual responsibility, tempered with a concern for less-well-off citizens. In 1961 Professor Dennis Lees wrote a farsighted Hobart Paper called *Health Through Choice*, which anticipated the general concern about the National Health Service only now re-awakened publicly. The NHS, with its attempt at universal provision of 'free' health care, stands at the core of the British welfare state. Yet it has constantly been in crisis. The publication of *Everyone a Private Patient* comes during one of the periodic eruptions of intense public debate about the state of the NHS.

This Foreword takes up some themes which Dr David Green addresses and which have arisen in the public debate over the NHS. The first surrounds its funding, which is a central theme of Dr Green's analysis. The NHS today is in the midst of a financial crisis — wards are closing, waiting lists lengthening, the staff demoralised. Some commentators blame the doctors and nurses, others the management or government. The truth is not a diplomatically weighted average of these accusations. There is no suggestion that doctors, nurses, administrators or any others connected with the NHS have deliberately contrived this situation. They are all responding to the incentives and constraints which form today's NHS. They are the pawns in a greater drama which will become self-perpetuating if radical reform is not undertaken.

As Dr Green cogently points out, there is an inherent contradiction in the NHS. Without prices and direct consumer payment for medical care, demand will exceed supply, costs will rise and resources will be misallocated.

His discussion points to two other drawbacks surrounding the NHS's monopoly. The first is the way alternative forms of providing health care have been suppressed. The second is the limited flow of information available to patients which would enable them to make informed, responsible, personal choices about the type and quantity of health care they want. The system has become bureaucratic and run in the interests of the producer groups rather than the patient.

The general debate about health care has taken place at an emotional level. When a member of one's family is seriously ill, one wants the best medical care without a concern about its costs. This is not the issue. All serious proposals for NHS reform assume that emergency care and other catastrophic illness will continue to attract assistance. That assistance can come through private or public, market or non-market, provision. The claim that health is different from other goods and services is too often used as a foil, both to obscure the fact that a considerable amount of health care is subjective, and that the NHS does not treat everyone equally.

The level of service provided in an administered system such as the NHS does not make the patient king. Like all bureaucratic systems it gives higher service to those located in better areas, and to the ill and infirm who are more articulate. The NHS does not provide a service that conforms to its proclaimed ideals. The question that must be asked is whether the NHS in its present form can ever meet these ideals. Dr Green argues, in line with fundamental economic teaching, that it cannot.

The clamour for more money misses the central issue. The performance of an essential service cannot be measured by the amount of money spent on it. Nor would a prudent administrator, whether in the private sector or the NHS sector, try to solve the problem of excess demand coupled with grossly inefficient production by automatically allocating more funds.

He would first ask whether the service is giving *value for money*. It is clear that the NHS has massive pockets of inefficiency which are slowly being reduced. No business can be run without proper accounting and cost control, and without everyone involved taking decisions in the light of the resources they consume by making those decisions. The issue is not more money, but who should pay and how it should be paid. And in answering these questions, the proper framework of analysis should be not that which offers immediate, temporary relief to a pressing cash-flow crisis, but the incentives promoting the efficient management, and allocation of resources to patient care which the different methods of funding have.

Dr Green puts forward a workable set of proposals designed to deal with the problems that the NHS now confronts. The solution is based on private, but government-assisted, insurance. If the funds come from private sources, where the patient has an element of choice, then costs must be competitive and a good service provided. While not all will agree with his detailed proposals, it must be acknowledged that they seek to tackle a difficult problem in a constructive way.

The Institute of Economic Affairs dissociates itself from the analysis and conclusions of its authors. Dr Green writes in his personal capacity, and his interpretation of the facts and conclusions are his own and not those of the IEA's Trustees, Advisers and Directors. His *Hobart Paperback* is nevertheless offered as an original contribution to public understanding of the economic analysis and practice of medical care, which has too long been neglected in the mostly political discussion over 40 years of the increasingly failing NHS. *Everyone a Private Patient* provides valuable information on the operation of health insurance schemes and a positive agenda for the introduction of health insurance into Britain's health system.

April 1988   CENTO VELJANOVSKI

PREFACE

Dr David G. Green
Director, IEA Health Unit

COULD Britain improve upon the National Health Service?
For most of its 40-year life the majority of people would
probably have answered with a resounding 'No'. In the last few
months, however, public confidence has sharply diminished
and many who once took the adequacy of the NHS for granted
now ask whether we could not do better. I have become convinced that Britain's health-care services would be significantly
improved if we switched to an insurance-based system. This
paper explains why and tries to come to terms with the not
inconsiderable problems involved in making health insurance
markets work well.

Debates about British health care have in the past tended to
be rather unproductive because of the notion that there are
really only two standpoints, collectivism or the free market, and
the Institute of Economic Affairs has frequently been associated with advocacy of the latter view. IEA authors have
certainly been convinced of the advantages that a competitive
market in insurance as well as medical services would bring for
the consumer, but have also recognised with no less firmness
that government must play a major role in maintaining access
for the poor and in ensuring that competition is not artificially
obstructed by providers.

However, the necessity for government intervention of some
sort does not mean that the function of government should
remain exactly as it is today. It is common to identify three

main roles that government can perform. It may *regulate* production by laying down rules; it may *finance* production by subsidising either prices or incomes (cash transfers); or it may directly *produce* goods or services. A fourth could be added, *publishing* information to assist consumers in making choices. For 40 years governments have both *financed* and *produced* services through the NHS, and I will argue that this all-embracing therapy has had inescapable side-effects that now call for a radical remedy.

Finally, may I thank colleagues who have read and commented on earlier drafts of the Paper: Rudolf Klein, Peter Collison, Robert Pinker, Sir Reginald Murley, George Teeling Smith, Michael Beesley, Cento Veljanovski and Graham Mather. Particular thanks go to Mike Solly, Ralph Harris and Arthur Seldon.

April 1988   DAVID G. GREEN

THE AUTHOR

DAVID G. GREEN was educated at the University of Newcastle upon Tyne, 1970-73, where he studied Political Science and Sociology. Whilst a postgraduate he lectured part-time on politics and sociology at Newcastle upon Tyne Polytechnic. He was a (Labour) councillor on Newcastle city council, 1975-81. From 1981 to 1983 he was a Research Fellow at the Australian University, Canberra. Since 1986 he has been Director of the Health Unit at the IEA.

Dr Green is the author of *Power and Party in an English City* (Allen & Unwin, London, 1980); (with L. Cromwell) *Mutual Aid or Welfare State* (Allen & Unwin, Sydney, 1984); *Working Class Patients and the Medical Establishment* (Gower/Temple Smith, London, 1985); and *The New Right: The Counter-Revolution in Political, Social and Economic Thought* (Wheatsheaf Books, Brighton, 1987). The IEA has published his *The Welfare State: For Rich or For Poor?* (1982), *Which Doctor?* (1985), *Challenge to the NHS* (1986), and *Medicines in the Marketplace* (1987). His work has also been published in *The Journal of Social Policy, Political Quarterly, Philosophy of the Social Sciences, Policy and Politics*.

INTRODUCTION
AND SUMMARY

ATTEMPTING both to finance and supply health-care services through the NHS has given rise to two fundamental problems: endemic underfunding and inadequate competition.

Reliance on Taxation has Caused Endemic Underfunding

There is widespread attachment to the NHS on ethical grounds because access to medical care is ranked with food, clothing and shelter as one of the essentials which everyone should enjoy in a civilised society, regardless of ability to pay. And most people support the NHS because they believe it guarantees them access to health-care services when they fall ill. It is increasingly being recognised, however, that in practice the NHS is not always there when it is needed. Some say the solution is for the government to give more money to the NHS, but in Chapter 1 I will suggest that this remedy will bring only temporary relief because the NHS has a serious structural flaw, namely, that it lacks any link between demand and budgetary allocation. So long as health services are supplied free at the time of use and financed out of taxes, governments will always find themselves confronting not priced demand but unpriced expectations, uninhibited by contemplation of the other goods and services, like housing and education, which might have been enjoyed instead.

Government funding is sometimes justified on the ground that medical 'need' can be measured and appropriate resources allocated. I will argue that the weakness of this claim is that a good deal of what goes on in hospitals is a matter of personal choice. Health care is a necessity when, for instance, someone has a broken limb or is bleeding or unable to breathe, or otherwise unstable. But there is no urgency about much health care. The risks involved in drug-taking or surgery must be weighed against benefits, and cost in time and money will also be a factor as decisions are made about which treatment, if any, is advisable. Much health care is not very different from other consumer goods which we consume, or refrain from consuming, because of the cost or personal preference. And certainly there is no finite quantum of 'need' which governments can measure.

Inevitably, governments relying on taxation to satisfy public expectations have to limit expenditure. The hospital service is given a cash-limited budget. Family practitioner spending, which includes drugs as well as the services provided by GPs, dentists and opticians, accounts for a little in excess of one-fifth of the NHS budget, but is not yet cash limited, though the Treasury would dearly like it to be. Expenditure on drugs, which absorbs about 46 per cent of family practitioner committee spending, is, however, subject to price control under the Pharmaceutical Price Regulation Scheme.[1] The result of a cash-limited hospital service has been waiting lists and the outright denial of treatment.

If we truly want each citizen to enjoy guaranteed access to a well-defined set of essential health-care services, regardless of their ability to pay, then this objective could be more effectively accomplished if each person had a contract of insurance setting out his or her entitlements. But such a contract can be offered only if the actuarially sound insurance premium has been paid, whether wholly by the patient or, if poor, for him or her by the state. It goes without saying that the government must continue to fund health care for the poor to an acceptable standard.

I then turn to the four main criticisms made of health insurance: (1) that it makes control of costs harder; (2) that it is more expensive to administer than the NHS (this is really a variant of the argument that health insurance is incapable of containing costs); (3) that consumers are too ill-informed to exercise choice; and (4) that it will lead to a 'two-tier' system

---

[1] Green (1987).

because the poor will get an inferior residual service financed by government.

Chapter 2 considers the claim that consumer ignorance makes a market unworkable and Chapters 3 and 4 discuss the record of health insurers in containing costs. The danger of a two-tier system developing is dealt with in Chapter 6.

Tax Finance Impedes Competition and Obstructs Human Ingenuity

The NHS has also impeded competition. The vast majority of people have only so much disposable income and because they are forced to pay for the monopolistic NHS they are not able to choose alternative provision. The absence of competition encourages bad service, as the government itself recognises; and, no less important, it discourages innovation and diversity.

A recurring theme throughout the study will be that there is virtue in diversity. American health care does not offer a ready-made blueprint, and this is still more obvious of the continental national insurance schemes. It does not matter where you look in the world, there is no obvious right answer. Problems remain and perverse incentives persist whether hospitals are paid a daily rate, or per case or unit of service, or are required to live within a global budget set by government; or whether doctors are paid a salary, capitation fee, fee per item of service, or per case. The conclusion I draw is that there is no point in searching for a single 'correct' solution. On the contrary, there is merit in variety.

A competitive market allows many ideas to be tried out at once, creating growing room for human ingenuity, so that if one answer does not work well there will always be something to compare it with, and alternatives to which consumers can turn for better service. Because it is a monopoly, the NHS not only denies people access to alternatives, but also conceals from them the information required to form a rational judgement about the quality of service they are getting. Greater competition affects:

(i) the *providers* which enter the market — helping to ensure that those which prosper are the ones that satisfy consumers;

(ii) the *products/services* which are offered — those least

3

attractive to consumers in terms of quality or performance tend to get eliminated; and

(iii) the *prices* at which services are sold — generally it encourages lower prices.

It must also be recognised that competition may produce perverse incentives and outcomes, a problem to which I turn in Chapter 6.

Critics of markets assert that competition leads, not to diversity, but to monopoly, and if true, this would be a decisive objection. But the evidence does not support this claim. If we look at America, for instance, monopoly power has not been the inevitable outcome.[1] On the contrary, and especially in the last 10 years, diversity has been the norm. And this variety has provided us with the international comparisons which enabled us to see that the NHS was not the best in the world. Health maintenance organisations (HMOs), for instance, have caught the imagination of many health policy analysts and it has been said that we should introduce HMOs within the NHS while continuing to rely on tax finance. It is important to recognise that those commentators who advocate the introduction of HMOs within the NHS are able to hold this view only because the health market-place in America allowed HMOs to develop and grow. If there had been an American national health service, HMOs would never have emerged for British policy-makers to admire.

There is a measure of decentralisation within the NHS, allowing some room for new ideas to be tried out, but there is nothing to resemble the trial and error of the free market. The NHS is over-centralised because its founders misunderstood how change and improvement occur. For instance, before the NHS was established there were already a number of non-profit medical aid associations providing primary medical care in a manner not dissimilar from modern HMOs, and they asked the government to allow them to continue their work as part of, or at least alongside, the NHS. One of them happened to be in Anthony Eden's constituency and he wrote to Aneurin Bevan drawing attention to their pioneering work.

---

[1] For an assessment of the evidence, Green (1986).

He was told that the Ministry realised the 'splendid work' of the medical aid associations, but the reason their services would no longer be required when the NHS got under way was

'simply that provision by public organisation and from public funds will have caught up with pioneer voluntary effort'.[1]

This reflected the feeling at the time that the NHS was the last word in the development of health services and that, therefore, there was no need to allow further room for private pioneering.

Personal Responsibility Undermined

Perhaps the most damaging effect of the NHS promise of 'free' health care has been the way it has undermined the capacity of people for self-direction, and spread a child-like dependency on the state. The deception involved in compelling people to pay for a monopoly service whilst at the same time presenting that service as a kind of gift from government has been part and parcel of the welfare state since its early origins before the First World War, when Lloyd George used the specious slogan 'ninepence for fourpence' to encourage support for the 1911 National Insurance Act. Male contributions were fourpence, employers threepence and the government twopence, and people were encouraged to think of the additional fivepence as a gift. But a tax on employers is a tax on jobs, and governments do not have any money of their own, only other people's. Personal payment cannot be escaped, but we can choose whether the payment takes the *form* of a tax or a freely-paid price. Paying a price is a *disposal* of income, whereas a tax is a *deduction from* income which takes away personal responsibility for deciding how much money will go into health care and curtails personal responsibility for selecting the best arrangements for the supply of medical services.

Dependency also has wider, less tangible, effects. In recent years the reforming spirit of the Government has been

---

[1] Public Record Office: PRO MH77/93; for a fuller discussion, D.G. Green, *Which Doctor?*, Research Monograph 40, London: IEA, 1985.

dominated by the necessity to face the economic facts of life. This was essential, but a civilised society cannot be built on economic policy alone. And if the recent economic revival is to be more than a respite from the post-war decades of decline we must seek to bring about a deeper rejuvenation of the cultural heritage that once meant that British ideas were admired throughout the world. The foundation stone of this culture was a spirit of self-direction. Parents freely accepted an obligation to provide for the important requirements of their children, including health care and education, and to raise them as good citizens. All but a minority of criminals and ne'er-do-wells freely accepted that right conduct was a personal duty to be fulfilled even when no one else was looking. But this independent spirit has been eroded by the welfare state ethic which said, not as collectivists insist, that people should help the unfortunate (an obligation in any event willingly accepted in Britain for centuries), but rather that everyone was a victim of circumstance, or 'the system'. And because we were all considered to be products of the environment all important services were to be provided by the state.

Ultimately this dependence on government undermines the chief foundation of a free society, the willingness of people freely to restrain their own exercise of freedom so that others may also enjoy it. As J.S. Mill clearly foresaw, by promising to provide for every important want, governments diminish opportunities for people to acquire the 'moral, intellectual and active' skills needed for self-rule. His objection to state intervention was not only that governments might provide some services less well than a competitive market, but also that, even if a government might carry out a function more effectively, we might still prefer it to be performed by voluntarily associating individuals

> 'as a means to their own mental education – a mode of strengthening their active faculties, exercising their judgement and giving them a familiar knowledge of the subjects with which they are thus left to deal'.

He also thought this might have the advantage of taking individuals 'out of the narrow circle of personal and family selfishness . . . habituating them to act from public or semi-public motives' and of teaching them to 'guide their conduct by aims which unite instead of isolating them from one another'.[1]

---

[1] Mill (1972), p. 164; (1970), p.312.

INSURANCE
OR TAXATION?

W HY, in the 1940s, did it seem reasonable to finance health-care services from taxation? When the NHS was established, ill-health was seen as an objective phenomenon which could be diagnosed by doctors on scientific grounds. People had in mind accidental injuries like broken limbs, or diseases like tuberculosis. Ill-health was also thought largely to be about life and death or, at least, the prevention of severe disability. It, therefore, seemed fundamental that no one should go without health care because they could not pay. And in the collectivist mood of the war years, there was wide agreement that the best way to ensure that everyone enjoyed access was to pay for health services from taxation.

**Everything that Can be Done should be Done —
Free at the Time of Use**

Thus, two notions formed the basis of our thinking about the NHS in its first 40 years: 'Everything that medically can be done should be done', and 'Everything should be free at the time of use'. These ideas are now under challenge. Increasingly it is being appreciated that ill-health is not a purely objective phenomenon, but rather that there is often an element of subjective consumer preference about both clinical and non-clinical decisions. Consequently, attempting to finance everyone's expectations about health care from taxation has proved impossible, because the government faces not an objective need, nor even priced demand, but rather unpriced expectations. The result is that the NHS fails to achieve the one objective which explains why it commands such wide support: guaranteeing access to all, regardless of ability to pay.

There is no finite pool of ill-health as was once thought. In the 1930s when the NHS was first conceived the main threats were from diseases such as tuberculosis, polio, or diphtheria and it was possible to think in terms of their eradication. Hence Beveridge's assumption that the NHS would pay for itself. But health-care problems today are of a different order. Modern transplant surgery, for instance, and the sophisticated 'high-tech' diagnostic equipment now available were undreamt of in the 1930s.

There is no absolute medical 'need' and no obviously correct treatment which matches every condition. There are often several alternative ways of treating a particular patient, each with its own advantages and disadvantages. Every such decision includes non-medical elements, such as cost (in terms of time and money), the patient's preference for this or that degree or type of risk, and the patient's willingness to cope with more or less pain or inconvenience. A particular surgical procedure may, for instance, carry a 5 per cent risk of death or increased disability. One person may decide it is not worth it, while another may decide to take a chance. The taking of drugs is a no less risky matter.[1] And diagnostic testing is not straightforward. If you are over 35 and pregnant you will be offered an amniocentesis test to detect disability in your child. For older women there is a 1-in-100 chance of having a disabled child, but the amniocentesis test carries a risk that a healthy child will die through miscarriage, also of one in 100. A second test is also available, chorionic villous sampling, but this carries a still higher risk of miscarriage of about one in 20. No one but the expectant parents can make the decision about whether or not to have such tests.

Thus, health care is partly (though not exclusively) like other consumer goods. To the extent that it is like other goods, funding from taxation is inappropriate.

Loss of Faith in the Scientific Credentials of Medicine

Faith in scientific progress and the value of scientific medicine

---

[1] Green (1987).

has formed the backdrop to much thinking about health care this century. Medical science is thought to have brought about 'miracle cures' and has been expected to continue the conquest of human disease. From this attitude it followed that health care was unquestionably desirable. If a doctor thought you needed medical care, it was good for you and you should have it. And money should be no obstacle.

Generally, it was believed that scientific progress would be made in the laboratories of the medical schools and that medical frontiers would be advanced in the teaching hospitals. Gradually, the lessons learnt there would spread to lesser institutions. Organisationally, this view meant that the top consultants should dictate priorities, as indeed they have since the inception of the NHS. During the 1970s, however, this consensus began to be questioned. First, confidence in the scientific credentials of medicine began to be challenged. Second, excessive professional power began to draw criticism.

Ivan Illich's *Limits to Medicine*, published as a Penguin paperback in 1977, was influential for a time. It began with the words:

'The medical establishment has become a major threat to health. The disabling impact of professional control over medicine has reached the proportions of an epidemic'.

Illich was an outsider, but there were also critics within medicine. In 1972 A.L. Cochrane, an epidemiologist, published his influential study of effectiveness and efficiency within the NHS. He found that increased financial input since the start of the NHS had not been matched by an equivalent increase in benefits for patients. And he cited several examples of the 'inefficient use of effective therapies, and considerable use of ineffective ones'.[1] He urged greater efforts to improve the scientific evaluation of medical treatment.

No less influential was Thomas McKeown. In *The Role of Medicine* (first published in 1976), he told how two things struck him during his time in a London teaching hospital:

'One was the absence of any real interest among clinical teachers in the origin of disease . . . the other was that whether

---

[1] Cochrane (1972), p. 67.

the prescribed treatment was of any value to the patient was often hardly noticed, particularly in internal medicine'.[1]

He thought that accident surgeons did a lot of good, as did obstetricians, with exceptions, but he had doubts about most other specialties. We have subsequently become more aware that medical intervention may inadvertently do more harm than good.

The high status of doctors, due chiefly to their association with the achievements of modern science, re-inforced their efforts to monopolise medical decision-making. Their power drew effective criticism, especially from American health economists, long used to directing their fire at monopolists in industry. Such critics made their mark on American policy-making from the mid-1970s onwards, as, one by one, the restrictive practices of the medical profession were declared unlawful.[2]

Cost is Always a Factor in Medical Decisions

There is a tendency to think of all health care as if it were emergency care, but much medical treatment is not urgent. Some conditions can safely remain untreated for two or three months, some a year and some longer still. Several conditions, like certain sporting injuries, cure themselves if left untreated. Haemorrhoids, a source of amusement to all but sufferers, can be treated surgically, but if left alone combined with a change of diet, may well clear up. There is often considerable personal discretion in respect of the timing of medical treatment. A person may, for instance, be suffering pain from an arthritic hip but because artificial joints tend to work loose over time, it may be advisable to delay replacement so that a second operation can be avoided in later years. Again, this is a personal preference to be exercised in the light of medical advice.

It is also important to recognise that the cost of treatment must be a factor in all medical decisions. There is a lingering feeling that sordid consideration of cost should have nothing to do with medical care, but the cost of care is always a factor which cannot be escaped. The only question is *who* decides. If

---

[1] McKeown (1979 edn.), pp. xi-xii.
[2] Green (1986).

patients do not weigh benefit against cost then the decisions will be made for them by the medical authorities.

Britain is not alone in having to face up to the lack of realism in the way we think about health care. Many countries, including Germany and America, operated for a time on the 'everything possible' principle and they too are having to rethink their attitudes, although the problems they have encountered are different from Britain's. Because health care is financed by national and private insurance respectively, and is therefore 'demand' led to a greater extent, expenditure in Germany and America has become disturbingly high. The emphasis in such countries is now on cost containment. In Britain, government has been able to impose an arbitrary ceiling on total expenditure and thus to curtail total outlays. But the cost has been borne by people on waiting lists or those who have been denied treatment outright, some of whom have died as a result.

Should There be *Any* Limit on Health Spending?

The nature of the problem can be seen if we ask the elementary question: Should there be *any* limit on health spending? If it is financed from taxes, for instance, should governments give the medical authorities whatever they say is necessary? Most people can see immediately that there can be no such open-ended commitment, but if there is to be a limit, who should decide what it should be? Since for the great majority of people, the money will come from their own pockets, either as taxes or insurance premiums, it seems reasonable that people should decide how much of their own money to spend on health. Taxation, however, provides no mechanism by which people can indicate how much they wish to assign to health care. They do not even know how much of their taxation is going into the NHS.

National insurance might appear preferable if *total* health-care spending was financed from national insurance contributions. The national insurance contribution, if separately identified on pay slips, would seem more like a price than a tax, but overseas governments have rarely been able to resist the temptation to subsidise health care partly from taxes. Thus, an earmarked tax or national insurance contribution has not in any country proved a watertight solution.

Private insurance is an imperfect mechanism but it does enable people to determine what proportion of their family budget should be spent on medical care. Most people will be able to pay their own way in the insurance market, but it goes without saying that government must provide for the poor who cannot help themselves, as I will argue in Chapter 6. The chief difficulty in evaluating the merits of private health insurance is that the largest insurance market, the USA, is also distorted by government intervention in the form of an imprudent and open-ended tax subsidy. The subsidy goes to workplace health plans and many employers pay all or a major part of each employee's health insurance premiums. The result is that employers face in microcosm many of the problems that the British government confronts. Examination of the American market does not, therefore, tell us exactly what a competitive insurance market with cost-conscious consumers would look like. But, nonetheless, we can learn a great deal about how markets work even when distorted by government subsidy.

Personal Responsibility

The question I ask, therefore, is: How can we maximise the extent to which individuals are able to take personal responsibility for health-care decisions? Such decisions fall into two groups. First, there are clinical decisions, about whether or not to undergo treatment at all, and if so, what type. The pattern in the past has been for the doctor's word to be gospel, but this is now changing as patients demand a more participatory doctor/patient relationship in which the risks and benefits of various alternative treatments are discussed. This development should be encouraged by putting doctors under a legal obligation (preferably by means of a patients' bill of rights) to seek the patient's fully informed consent to treatment.[1] It is essential that patients' rights to information are not forgotten in the concern to reform the funding of health-care services.

Second, there are financial decisions, about how to pay for health care. Insurance is the only realistic alternative to taxa-

---

[1] For a discussion of the doctrine of 'informed consent', Green (1987).

tion, though it can be advantageous for consumers to rely in part on out-of-pocket payment.

When choosing an insurance policy, judgements have to be made about the type and extent of coverage. There is a huge variety of insurance plans, as I will explain in Chapter 3. For instance, a person may choose the relatively comprehensive coverage of a health maintenance organisation (to which subscribers pay a fixed monthly premium in return for all necessary health-care services without any further obligation to pay fees). Alternatively, the consumer may choose a preferred provider organisation, which reduces costs by encouraging the use of approved (preferred) hospitals, believed to be more efficient. Or an indemnity plan may be selected, with no limits on choice of doctor but, in return for a lower premium, offering cover above a certain floor, or only up to a certain ceiling. Plans with a 'deductible' provide for consumers to meet, say, the first £500 of all bills in a year, after which they are covered for further expenditure. The ceiling may be, perhaps, £250,000 a year. Co-insurance, requiring the consumer to pay, say, 20 per cent of doctors' bills, may also form part of the policy. As with other insurance, the more the consumer pays small expenses out of pocket the lower the insurance premium. Thus, consumers can weigh the extent of their coverage against their expenditure on premiums, trading one for the other.

Many will initially hesitate at the idea of people being free to take out insurance policies for less than comprehensive cover, so that cost will be a factor if they fall ill. As I have already argued, this reaction is based on a mistaken view that all health care is equally urgent. But more than this, there is a tendency to treat medical-care decisions as if they were in a separate compartment from other choices we make which have a no less significant impact on our health status, including our prospects for survival. People may, for instance, choose to smoke, risking lung cancer; drink alcohol, risking liver damage; or consume an unhealthy diet, leading to obesity and heart failure. Or they may enjoy hang-gliding, mountain-climbing or pot-holing precisely because of the risk. If we are free to smoke or participate in dangerous sports, then why should we not be free to choose a health insurance policy which does not cover every conceivable treatment?

Figure 1
The Costs and Benefits of Medical Spending

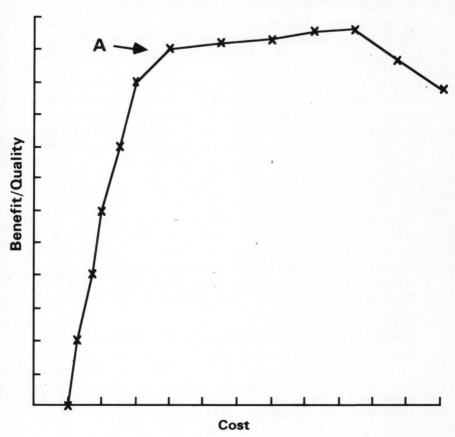

More important still, we must recognise that it may be entirely rational to choose only to finance medical services up to a specified point. Above a certain level of spending, health care does not necessarily produce benefits. It produces diminishing returns and may even be counter-productive. This can be seen clearly in Figure 1. Spending above point A in Figure 1 is commonly called expenditure on 'flat-of-the-curve'

15

medicine. Electronic foetal heart monitoring provides an example. When an expectant mother enters hospital to give birth an electronic instrument is inserted into the unborn infant's scalp to detect foetal distress which could cause disability or death. When distress is discovered a decision may be taken to deliver the baby by Caesarian section, and the growth of foetal heart monitoring may explain the increase in the use of Caesarian sections in recent years.

But there are risks associated with the use of foetal heart monitoring, including injuries to the foetal scalp, infection, and distress resulting from the monitoring itself. There are further risks associated with Caesarian section. Authoritative studies, including one carried out at Harvard Medical School, have cast doubt on the value of foetal heart monitoring.[1] Births were placed in one of five risk categories, according to the predicted likelihood of complications developing. It was discovered that for deliveries with a low risk of complications, foetal heart monitoring did more harm than good. For high-risk births, however, it helped. Thus, monitoring high-risk births is justified, but monitoring them all is harmful. The difficulty is deciding what degree of risk should be monitored and at what point expenditure on foetal heart monitoring is not only unnecessary but harmful. Such judgements are difficult but inescapable.

Low Spending — A Reason for Regret or Celebration?

I have said that the outcome of reliance on taxation has been underfunding. I did so because the experience of other countries shows that if we switched to a funding system which gave individuals more control over how much to spend on health care, Britain's spending would undoubtedly rise. Some commentators complain that a lot of health-care spending is unnecessary and that downward budgetary pressure on doctors is not only inevitable but a good thing. According to Professor Julian Le Grand, for example, the fact that Britain devotes a relatively small share of GDP to health care is a 'cause for celebration, not complaint'.[2]

---

[1] Neutra *et al.* (1978), pp. 324-26.
[2] Le Grand (1988).

He argues this because mortality statistics for other nations which spend more on health care than Britain are not very different from our figures and because he believes some, perhaps much, medical care to be ineffective or even harmful. The NHS, he says, 'is an excellent instrument for curbing wasteful health spending'. His first argument, that mortality rates in advanced nations are quite similar despite substantial differences in the amount spent on health care, is his weakest. Much health care is not about life-threatening conditions and therefore mortality statistics should not be expected to reveal very much about the performance of a health-care system. His second contention, that the effectiveness of much health care is, at best, uncertain is soundly based, as we have already seen. And a strict limit on total spending may well discourage such medical interventions. But does it in practice?

In countries like America and Germany there has almost certainly been huge spending on what is called 'flat-of-the-curve' medicine. In Britain, although spending per head is lower, this sort of spending has also occurred. If we look at the activities of NHS doctors, we find that a good deal of 'ineffective medicine' (perhaps one should say, 'unproven medicine') is carried out. The authors (themselves doctors) of a recent report on deaths resulting from surgery, for example, criticised some of their colleagues for unnecessary and point-less surgical interventions.[1] And NHS hospital consultants are as enthusiastic as their overseas colleagues about glamorous techniques and shiny new equipment which may or may not be of much help to the patient. One of the reasons that waiting lists for routine operations like hernias or varicose veins are so long is that doctors prefer to spend NHS budgets on exciting high technology medical care or 'interesting' cases, instead of on services actually demanded by their patients.

Thus, there is strong support for Le Grand's argument that downward budgetary pressure can be desirable and by implication that medical standards do not necessarily suffer if doctors are required to be cost-conscious. But are the incentives doctors face under the NHS the best way of bringing a climate of cost-consciousness without cutting corners at the

---

[1] Buck, Devlin, and Lunn (1987).

patient's expense? Two conditions are necessary to ensure that cost-cutting does not harm patients. The first is that people should be free to determine how much of their own money to put into health care. And second, there must be competition, so that if a particular doctor or institution cuts corners, people can go elsewhere and avoid being trapped in a bad service. The NHS fails on both these counts. A private insurance system allows people the flexibility to influence the total budget within which doctors must act and the power to choose alternatives when dissatisfied.

There is instinctive mistrust of private competitive markets because they are associated with the profit motive. But advocacy of a competitive market does not imply approval only of the profit motive. It is an appeal to set free all lawful human motivations, including self-help (personal responsibility for self and family), mutual aid (shared obligation towards oneself and others beyond the family), and charity (a sense of duty towards strangers who are not expected to give anything in return). Profit-making institutions would certainly exist, but the evidence from British and overseas history is that in a market non-profit institutions tend to dominate.[1] Before national insurance was enacted in 1911, some three-quarters of the working population were in mutual aid societies providing sick pay and primary medical care guided by the philosophy that people should band together to help one another in hard times.[2] Moreover, until 1948 most people received their hospital care from voluntary hospitals financed by charitable contributions and voluntary pay-packet deductions and built up on an ethic of serving the sick. This ethic was not empty rhetoric, but a reality which explains why, *before* the NHS, it was common for people to speak of British health care as the 'envy of the world'. It can, therefore, be claimed without exaggeration that the free market invented the non-profit hospital. Under the NHS, however, the spirit of service nurtured in the non-profit voluntary hospitals has steadily evaporated.

Thus, the NHS may exert downward pressure on spending. But the ceiling is arbitrarily determined and the decisions

---

[1] Green (1985).
[2] This mutual aid tradition is described in Green (1985).

made within restricted budgets by doctors bear no relationship to the declared objective of limiting the use of ineffective
procedures.

Insurance Premiums or Taxes?

There are three basic ways of financing health care: taxation,
out-of-pocket payment, and insurance. In practice, the high
cost of much medical care means that there are only two main
alternatives, taxation and insurance. So far I have argued that
reliance on taxation has meant that governments must set a
limited NHS budget, which has led inevitably to rationing
through waiting lists and the denial of treatment. For many
years this rationing problem was not openly acknowledged.
Patients were denied treatment and told by the doctors that
they were sorry but there was nothing medical science could
do for them, whereas the reality was that decisions to give or
withhold treatment depended upon budget allocations which
were in part the product of intra-professional rivalry, as this
or that consultant fought for resources from other departments. Thus, decisions resulting from budget limitation were
concealed by disguising them as clinical judgements.

For most of the life of the NHS, doctors co-operated with
this profoundly immoral deception of patients with the result
that political and academic supporters of the NHS were able
to disregard the inevitability of rationing. Today, doctors
increasingly refuse to mask the NHS reality and NHS loyalists
have been compelled to acknowledge that there must be a
fixed global budget and that this will mean medical rationing.
They still, however, oppose the alternative of insurance and
urge only that we must make NHS rationing more efficient.
Orthodox health economists accept that at present NHS
resource allocation results from the arbitrary pushing and
shoving which occurs as rival departments in each hospital vie
for funds, and they single out for criticism the consultants,
who are said to be insufficiently accountable. Some spend
heavily on new technology, while others persist in the use of
outdated or ineffective techniques without regard to cost or
the benefit to patients. However, academics like Professors
Maynard and Williams, at the University of York, contend
that the solution is, not insurance, but to put rationing
decisions on a more technical footing using Quality Adjusted

Life Years (QALYs). Essentially, the value of an additional year of each person's life is given a numerical value by researchers and if an individual's score relative to others is low, he will be denied treatment and, if seriously ill, allowed to die. The quality of life of a person undergoing renal dialysis, for instance, is thought to be rather poor, and in the view of Professor Maynard, treatment should be withheld in order that others should be treated who can live higher quality lives.

The objection to this process of resource allocation is that it regards medical judgements, including life and death decisions, as a purely technical matter, with the victim excluded from the decision process. But its advocates cannot be faulted for their intellectual honesty. Gone is the wishful thinking of the early years of the NHS, and gone is the immorality of pretending that all decisions were purely clinical. Under a QALY system, doctors would no longer make rationing decisions and pretend that they were making a clinical judgement. Decisions to give or withhold medical treatment would be taken out of the hands of top consultants and made according to a person's value in a statistical table. I venture to suggest that if Aneurin Bevan had foreseen this development he would have been in favour of financing health care from insurance premiums.

I now turn to an examination of how insurance markets function, including an analysis of how the complex and difficult moral dilemmas involved in cost-containment are handled.

Is Health Care Different?

The first obstacle to be surmounted in judging whether health insurance is a realistic alternative to tax finance is the claim made by some economists that health care is so different that an efficient competitive market in health insurance is impossible to achieve. Economists have traditionally adopted three main approaches when considering the public/private mix in health care.

1. They have drawn up lists of 'market failures' which are presumed to justify government intervention. Such lists have taken two main forms. First, there have been catalogues of observed characteristics, such as the widespread presence of a monopolistic medical profession.

Second, some scholars have identified the 'inherent properties' of health care, from which the observable differences between health services and other commodities are considered to be derived. Insurance, for instance, is interpreted as a response to the unavoidable uncertainty surrounding the incidence of ill-health.

2. Economists have also contrasted existing health-care markets with a hypothetical ideal — perfect competition.

3. They have drawn attention to the inability of the poor to pay for essential health-care services, observed that the vast majority of people dislike this state of affairs, and concluded that the government may legitimately raise taxes from everyone to provide, not only for the needy, but also for the whole population. In one variant this approach is called the 'caring externality'[1] and, in another, the widespread public concern for the health of others is considered to be one of the inherent properties of health care.[2]

An example of the approach which lists observed differences is provided in a recent paper by Gray, Marinker and Maynard in the *British Medical Journal*.[3] In the short run they advocate 'good practice allowances' for primary care and in the longer term they favour the introduction of health maintenance organisations within the NHS, but they oppose any transition towards a competitive market because, they say, the market view 'bears little relation to the real world'.[4] In this 'real world', professional monopoly power enables doctors to maximise their income; patients lack the knowledge to function as sovereign consumers; and insurance mechanisms remove the incentives for providers and consumers to economise.

But, as Professor Kenneth Arrow recognised in his seminal study of health care published in 1963, it is important to distinguish between the *inherent* characteristics of health care

---

[1] Culyer and Posnett (1985).
[2] e.g. Evans (1984), p. 26.
[3] D. Gray, M. Marinker, and A. Maynard, 'The doctor, the patient, and their contract', *British Medical Journal*, 17 May 1986, pp. 1,313-5; 24 May 1986, pp. 1,374-6; 31 May 1986, pp. 1,438-40.
[4] *Ibid.*, p. 1,439.

and those differences between markets for health care and markets for other goods and services which can be *observed* at any given moment. Many visible problems may be remediable, whereas the inherent characteristics of health care must be accepted as given. Arrow identifies two such inherent properties. The special economic problems of medical care, he says, can be explained as adaptations to the existence of uncertainty about (a) 'the incidence of disease' and (b) 'the efficacy of treatment'. The features of health-care markets which have been described and studied by researchers should be seen as adaptations or 'social adjustments' to these *inherent* properties.[1] I will follow Arrow in distinguishing between given and derived characteristics, but I will add a third to his list, namely, that life-threatening health care has long been seen as a fundamental human requirement which ought not to be neglected. It is not an inevitable characteristic, but it is a sentiment so deeply entrenched that it can be regarded as a 'given' for all practical purposes.

Thus, I will accept that health care is different and that the differences appear to justify a remedial role for government. But the important question is, what should that role be, and, more specifically, is it advisable for government to play a role which goes beyond providing a remedy to *suppressing alternatives*? For instance, it is one thing for the government to accept that it must finance health care for the poor, but quite another to attempt to finance health care for everyone, with the result that most people are left with an income insufficient to contemplate expenditure on alternatives. The issue, therefore, is not 'government — right or wrong?', but whether the form of government intervention chosen in 1948, namely, public provision of all health care financed wholly from taxes, does more harm than good by putting obstacles in the way of alternatives.

I now turn to the specific objections made against health insurance compared with the NHS.

---

[1] Arrow (1963), p. 941.

CAN CONSUMERS CHOOSE?

'An economist is someone who tries to prove that what works in practice also works in theory, except in health care. Some health economists seek to prove that what works in practice cannot work in theory.'[1]

WITH these words Professor Alain Enthoven sums up the contribution of conventional economics to the analysis of health care. His assessment applies with special force to the work of British health economists on the ability of consumers to choose.

The argument that consumers of medical services are too poorly informed to exercise sovereign choice has taken two main forms. In one version the conclusion is derived from a comparison between reality and the theoretical model of perfect competition; and in the other, an asymmetry of information between doctor and patient is said to be one of the inherent properties of health care.

Perfect Competition and Consumer Choice

A common technique in economic analysis is to compare the real world with a hypothetical situation, perfect competition, a state of affairs which ensures optimal economic efficiency in the allocation of resources. Arrow's trail-blazing article[2] uses this technique of contrasting the real world with perfect competition, and it has been employed many times since, despite strong criticism from scholars such as Professor Culyer.[3] A recent example is provided by a new textbook on the economics of the welfare state by Nicholas Barr.[4] The starting point for Barr's

---

[1] Enthoven (1986), p. 114.
[2] Arrow (1963), *op. cit.*
[3] Culyer (1971), pp. 189-211.
[4] Barr (1987).

analysis is the economic model, perfect competition, the pre-conditions for which are:

1. So many sellers that no single one can influence the market price.

2. Perfect information on the part of buyers and sellers about alternatives or opportunities elsewhere.

3. The absence of significant economies of scale, so that no firm is likely to be dominant.

4. No artificial barriers to the movement of people or materials.

Barr then proceeds to examine health care in the real world to see whether the pre-conditions of perfect competition are met, insisting in particular that '*the advantages of competition are contingent on perfect information*'.[1] He finds that the perfect information requirement is not met, and concludes that greater competition is undesirable.

The disadvantage of this approach is that it starts with a model and finds reality wanting by comparison, whereas there is no reason why reality should conform to some hypothesised ideal. It is true that study of markets functioning in the real world confirms that no one has perfect information about the best products, the best providers, and the best prices. But, as Hayek taught, we also find that competition is useful precisely *because* it is a mechanism which improves and adds to the comparative information at people's disposal. Competition generates comparisons, enabling consumers to contrast prices as well as the quality of goods and services; whereas the opposite situation of monopoly suppresses comparisons, precisely to put consumers in a weak position. Information (perfect or otherwise) should not, therefore, be seen as a *pre-condition* of competition but rather as something which emerges as a *consequence* of it. Accordingly, it does not follow that because consumers are imperfectly informed competition is undesirable or unattainable.

The Information Asymmetry

According to Professor Arrow, there is uncertainty about how

---

[1] Barr, *op. cit.*, p. 300 (emphasis in original).

effective any required treatment will be, and the extent of the uncertainty faced by the consumer may differ from that of the doctor because of the doctor's greater knowledge. Today, it is more common to refer only to the asymmetry of information between doctor and patient. Professor Robert Evans, for instance, takes Arrow to task for using the term 'uncertainty' to refer to the 'unpredictability of illness' as well as the 'lack of consumer information about appropriate use'. They are, he says, very different. He suggests that there are three 'inherent' characteristics of health care: uncertainty about the incidence of illness, asymmetry of information between provider and consumer, and 'external effects' in consumption. From this 'fundamental triad', he says, 'all other listed characteristics can be derived'.[1]

But Arrow's conception is surely more accurate. For him the inherent characteristic was 'uncertainty about the effectiveness of treatment', a difficulty faced by both doctor and patient. He was conscious that uncertainty about the consequences and possibility of treatment differed between provider and consumer, although he felt that the extent of the asymmetry may have been overstated in the past.[2] He also regarded the fact that patients considered themselves to be less well informed than doctors to be the main concern for the student of actual human conduct. This is plainly true, but as I will argue in a moment, it is very important constantly to bear in mind that the uncertainty about effectiveness faces both doctor and patient and that the gap between the doctor's knowledge and the patient's knowledge will vary from case to case. Some patients with a long experience of medical treatment may become more knowledgeable than any given doctor, while the patient who, for instance, is taken suddenly ill will have no time to acquire information about alternatives.

Arrow also helped to clarify the nature of the difference between the doctor's knowledge and the patient's knowledge. Producers usually know more about production methods than consumers and medicine is no exception, but consumers of other goods and services are presumed to be the best judges of the value to them of alternative commodities. Doctors, it is

---

[1] Evans, *op. cit.*, p. 26.
[2] Arrow, *op. cit.*, p. 951, note 22.

said, are often in a better position than the patient to decide which among a range of alternative products (treatments) will be best for the patient. The consumer, therefore, is not the best judge. In practice, consumers of high-cost and long-lasting goods and services base their judgements on a manufacturer's reputation, a recommendation from a friend or other third party, or a personal survey of the products available. In medicine, reputation plays a similar part, as do second opinions and third-party endorsements, for instance when self-help or pressure groups press for a treatment like radical mastectomy for breast cancer to be abandoned, or a screening process like cervical smear testing to be extended. The extent of this difference between medicine and other products should not, therefore, be exaggerated. But the difficulty patients face in judging which among a range of alternatives would be in their best interests is important and the historical outcome has been the emergence of a doctor-patient relationship based on trust.

The 'Trust' Relationship

Arrow was particularly concerned that patients bore the cost of uncertainty about the effectiveness of medical treatment, and he thought that in a perfectly competitive market pro-ducers would be paid by results only and would take out insurance against the risk of failing to recommend the 'correct' treatment. The consequence would be that the cost of failure would be transferred from the patient to the doctor.[1] He observed that no such insurance emerged and, according to Professor Culyer, one of the main reasons is that it is often difficult to establish whether any given treatment has actually been successful.[2] As a result, instead of relying on mechanisms which transfer the cost of failure or the uncertainty from the patient to the doctor, who in turn insures, most societies, says Culyer, have evolved the special relationship of 'trust' between doctor and patient.

This is largely true, but alongside the 'trust' relationship has been the possibility of suing the doctor for failure. In America this practice has now reached such heights that the situation

---

[1] Arrow, *op. cit.*, p. 964.
[2] Culyer, *op. cit.*, p. 197.

must come close to Arrow's ideal of transferring the cost of failure from patient to doctor. Medical practitioners who fail to produce promised results are regularly sued and compelled to pay substantial damages. Naturally they carry insurance to protect themselves and are said to practice 'defensive medicine' because of their fear of being sued. In Britain, malpractice or medical negligence suits were very rare until recently, but in the last few years doctors have found themselves before the courts far more frequently and damage payments are rising sharply, as increases in the insurance premiums being paid by doctors to medical protection societies testify.

Thus, the relationship of trust, or deference to the doctor's judgement, has always been qualified and in recent times has come under considerable strain in America. In Britain the same process is under way as people shake off the dependency-inducing effects of decades of welfare statism and grow accustomed to controlling their own destinies. The trust relationship should not, therefore, be regarded as set in concrete. It is a consequence of the uncertainty surrounding the results of medical treatment, but is it the best we can do? How well have traditional institutions based on 'trust' served the consumer?

Does Professional Self-Regulation Protect Consumers?

The importance of the difference between Professor Arrow's conception of the properties of health care and Professor Evans' is that Arrow acknowledges that uncertainty about the effects of treatment is also faced by doctors. According to Evans, the information asymmetry makes it possible for doctors to exploit patients and, therefore, he concludes, 'regulation' has been and remains necessary. Regulation has taken the form of licensing of doctors by professionally dominated institutions, in Britain the General Medical Council (GMC). Has it protected the consumer from exploitation by doctors?

If Arrow is correct, the uncertainty facing all parties (including doctors) means that *doctors can mislead each other*, as well as patients, and it is this that puts the consumer in a weak position. It is always possible to get a second opinion, but across a wide range of procedures no doctor can make a final judgement that a particular medical intervention was either necessary or unnecessary, effective or ineffective. This explains why large differences in the rates of surgical intervention between regions have regularly been discovered by researchers. A great deal depends on personal judgement, influenced by local fashion or convention, and, according to a recent study by the Rand Corporation, there is also a significant amount of 'inappropriate' care (below, p. 44).

If this is the problem, then to opt for professional self-regulation as the principal means of protecting the consumer has the effect of putting the consumer in still greater danger because in practice self-regulation has made it easier for the profession to close ranks against outsiders. Controversies about the correctness of particular treatment régimes have been kept within the profession, with consumers excluded. This lack of open debate has encouraged the continued use of ineffective treatments and the lack of scientific evaluation of medical interventions to which reference was made in Chapter 1. In a competitive market, however, medical judgements inevitably containing a measure of discretion can more readily be exposed to contradiction by as many unbiased observers as possible.

Fortunately, there are alternatives to professional self-regulation which provide checks and balances to safeguard the consumer's interests. Insurance companies in America, for instance, frequently require pre-admission authorisation before they will agree to pay for hospitalisation, and compulsory second opinion programmes have the effect of exposing doctors' recommendations to challenge (Chapter 3). For many years HMOs have used such methods to discourage unnecessary treatments or the continued use of outmoded treatment régimes. Yet, economists who lay stress on the information asymmetry favour the continuation of the historically established method of protection by professional self-regulation even though it has obstructed the emergence of other methods of protecting patients.

Professional self-regulation has, for example, given organised medicine the power to impose restrictive practices that include a ban on advertising, which makes it harder for consumers to avoid falling into the hands of incompetent practitioners. For instance, if a group practice in Britain operated an efficient computerised recall system for women with irregular cervical smear test results, why should it not be free to draw the attention of potential customers to this fact and invite prospective patients to consider whether neighbouring group practices were equally well organised? Consider plastic surgery. When the British Association of Aesthetic Plastic Surgeons, which has about 120 members, receives an inquiry from a potential patient about whether the association has an accredited member in a particular area the GMC prevents the organisation even from sending out a full membership list, let alone recommending a local surgeon. The result is that people can, and do, fall into the hands of less scrupulous surgeons. In America in 1982 the Supreme Court declared unlawful the advertising ban enforced by the American Medical Association (AMA). The medical profession may now only interfere if advertising is untruthful. A similar development in Britain is long overdue.

It is also important to remember that the GMC does not certify the continuing competence of doctors. It says only that they have passed an approved examination at the beginning of their career. More than this, it authorises doctors to practise a range of skills in which they are not actually expected to be expert. Any doctor is licensed, for instance, to carry out open-heart surgery, but very few are capable of doing it. For this reason we should look upon licensing as government recognition of a group claim to monopolise a bundle of skills, as much as a device for protecting consumers. Of course, doctors who consider themselves badly informed on a given subject are supposed to refer patients to a specialist, but many British GPs are not well equipped to perform this role. They know few specialists, have little contact with hospitals, and tend to rely on the same hospital or person all or most of the time. Some 60 per cent of GPs' letters to consultants at a famous London teaching hospital, for instance, begin 'Dear Doctor', suggesting that GPs do not know the name of the specialist who will treat the patient they are referring. Under the NHS, GPs make little or no attempt to survey the field on the consumer's behalf.

It does not, therefore, make automatic sense to defend

institutions which presume a constant and substantial asymmetry of information and which presuppose that doctors are more competent across a wider range of skills than they are in reality.

Consumer Choice

The medical consumer is said to lack information about the consequences of treatment and because of this can be exploited by doctors. The consumer, in other words, is too ill-informed to be a good judge of his or her own interests. Consumers need to make several choices, including the timing of their treatment and the venue, but here I will focus on three main decisions: (1) choice between doctors; (2) choice between the recommendations of one or more doctors; and (3) choice between health insurance plans. Formally, the uncompetitive NHS allows patients at least two choices, to select their own GP and to give consent to surgery. But if it is their inability to judge the efficacy of any particular course of treatment which makes them incapable of exercising choice, then why allow people to withhold consent for treatment? If Barr's argument is followed to its logical extreme, patients should be instructed to undergo any treatment which doctors consider to be good for them. And why let them 'chop and change' from doctor to doctor, when they will do so on inadequate grounds?

Few analysts, however, would press the argument this far because they accept that patients may have valid reasons for not undergoing treatment; and few would insist that patients must be compulsorily assigned to GPs, because they accept that they may have sound reasons for changing doctor. Partly because in a given case the patient may know more than the doctor, and partly because doctors make mistakes, the freedom of consumers to choose their GP and refuse consent for treatment is regarded as an essential protection against exploitation. And if this is true, should we not search for ways of improving the consumer's ability to make such choices more effectively? More than this, if the institutions which historically have been put in place ostensibly to protect the consumer appear to have failed, or, worse still, have come to weaken the consumer's power, as advertising restrictions do, then should they not be replaced? And at the minimum, ought we to suppress the emergence of alternative institutions or mechanisms which are already known to assist consumers as they confront the risks they face in seeking medical care? I have in mind, not only devices like mandatory second surgical opinions, pre-admission authorisation and concurrent review (Chapter 3), currently being developed by American and some British insurance companies, but also the emergence of sophisticated groups of buyers.

Many American health-plan managers are developing skills in selecting doctors and hospitals according to their quality of service. Ryder System Inc., an international transport company with 37,000 employees whose health plan cost $23 million in 1986, provides an example. The company is self-insured and offers a traditional fee-for-service plan. In 1987 it introduced MedFacts to provide quality and cost information to help employees choose efficient doctors. For its head-quarters staff in Florida, for instance, MedFacts contains information about 4,000 doctors, including prices, education, current hospital affiliations, disciplinary actions outstanding, and training. Some hospitals are known to be more rigorous in granting hospital privileges and so hospital affiliation can be a useful indicator of standard of service. MedFacts data also reveal that there is no *necessary* link between price and quality. For instance, doctors with specialty board certification and American training charged less on average than foreign-trained, non-board certified doctors. Price differences were due to factors such as higher profit margins, higher overhead costs, and higher malpractice premium payments due to involvement in more claims than the average. This information enabled individual employees to avoid not only the more costly surgeons but also the least proficient.[1]

Choice of Doctor: Consumers in everyday markets now demand and expect good and courteous service from competing suppliers, and the low priority given by the NHS to serving consumers appears increasingly incongruous and unreasonable. For instance, instead of using an appointment system, some NHS hospitals are still calling in 10 or 12 people at 9.00 a.m., knowing full well that the last will not be seen

---

[1] Charles (1987), pp. 36-38.

until 12.00 noon or later. Under the NHS choice is deliberately restricted. Formally, people are free to change their GP when dissatisfied but in practice their choice is restricted in some localities.

Choice of surgeon is especially important. Yet, NHS hospitals offer no choice of surgeon. Patients are required to sign forms consenting to surgery but must also declare that they realise no undertaking is being given that any particular surgeon will carry out the operation. In surgery, practice makes perfect, and choosing someone who carries out a procedure regularly increases the patient's chances of survival by a significant margin. The Confidential Enquiry into Perioperative Deaths reviewed 151 deaths following surgery for peptic ulcers. The deaths were surgeon-related in over 31 per cent of cases and in over 9 per cent operations were performed by senior house officers, the most junior grade of trainee surgeon.[1] Surgeons are not all equally competent and, according to the Royal College of Surgeons, it is not uncommon for an inexperienced NHS surgeon to be 'thrown in at the deep end', especially in the handling of emergencies.[2] The Confidential Enquiry into Perioperative Deaths also found 10 cases of patients who had died after being taken to Accident and Emergency Departments which 'were not geared to the instant management of major trauma'. Assessors commented that five of the 10 people would probably have survived in an American or Continental trauma centre.[3]

In America useful mechanisms are emerging to assist consumers. HMOs and PPOs, described in Chapter 3, select their doctors' panels according to the price of their services, their utilisation review record (below, p.45) and their willingness to submit to quality assurance machinery, thus helping consumers to make informed choices. The NHS impedes the development of such institutions.

Some comparative data are now available to help consumers choose individual surgeons. The US Department of Health and Human Services has published the crude mortality rates of hospitals using data from Medicare peer review

---

[1] Buck *et al.* (1987), p. 53.
[2] Royal College of Surgeons (1986), p. 6.
[3] *Ibid.*, p. 55.

organisations, though such comparisons are in their infancy and must be used with caution.[1] Contrasting mortality and morbidity rates during surgery with the frequency a particular procedure is carried out by an individual hospital has proved a more useful indicator of hospital performance. The less frequently a hospital carries out a procedure, the more likely it is that patients will die or suffer post-operative infections.[2] American insurance companies are beginning to use this insight to enhance their pre-admission review procedures. Blue Cross in California, for example, will approve certain operations only in hospitals which have more than a certain throughput of patients, considered sufficient for surgeons to maintain their competence. About 150 operations a year are thought to be the minimum necessary for optimal performance.

The Joint Commission on Accreditation of Hospitals (JCAH) announced at the end of 1986 that it would begin incorporating clinical outcomes into its hospital accreditation process. It did so as a direct result of the new competitive environment. As the JCAH president put it: 'If we don't, others will'.[3] The Health Care Quality Improvement Act, 1986, requires the creation of a clearing-house on physician data, including details of hospital and state disciplinary actions, as well as particulars of doctors who have paid out in malpractice suits. Such access has been resisted by doctors, but the American courts are enforcing patients' rights to information.

The accreditation process, whereby American doctors are granted the right to admit patients to a particular hospital, provides a more rigorous check on doctors than anything the NHS offers. Records are kept in some hospitals, for example, of each surgeon's post-operative infection rate. If surgeons fail to come up to scratch, their privileges may be withdrawn.

Some of the developments mentioned have been initiated by government, and the evidence suggests that a continuing role for the state would be useful. The issue is not, therefore, 'the market versus the state' in some absolute sense but whether it

---

[1] HHS (1986).

[2] Greenberg (1984).

[3] *Hospitals*, 20 December 1986, p. 80.

is desirable to allow the continued suppression of such developments in Britain.

Consent to Treatment: There are occasions when the patient may be quite correct in declining treatment. Over-treatment, for instance, is not only confined to fee-for-service medicine. British GPs are known to over-use antibiotics and tranquillisers, some say to speed patients out of the door with the minimum of effort on the doctor's part. And research-oriented hospitals like to 'practise' on patients.

A demand for improved health status may lead to increased self-care, instead of reliance on medical intervention. The failure of orthodox medicine to cope adequately with some conditions may lead, *inter alia*, to the use of alternative practitioners. Conditions like back pain have been much improved by alternative practitioners like osteopaths and chiropractors. Orthodox doctors tend to rely on remedies like non-steroidal anti-inflammatory drugs which produce side-effects and may do little good. But the control of the GMC by organised orthodox medical practitioners tends to impede the development of alternatives and thus to suppress comparisons which may help consumers make more informed choices, as they decide whether or not to agree to this or recommended treatment.

Not so long ago there was a tendency to put medical practitioners on a pedestal. This is now changing, not only as a result of the growing awareness that medical intervention is of uncertain value, but also because of the rise of consumerism. Patient participation has been urged in order to dilute professional dominance, and a patients' bill of rights has been advocated by more than one organisation. The lead has been taken by women who have objected to the regimentation of childbirth by professionals. They have demanded less reliance on 'high-tech' gadgetry and drugs and more emphasis on 'natural' childbirth, as well as a right to give birth in the home.

Choice of Health Plan: The consumer is said to be a less competent judge than the doctor of the likely value to him of a particular treatment or range of treatments. This difficulty affects the doctor/patient relationship, as we have seen, but it is also used as an argument against competition between private health insurers. Yet it has little bearing on the consumer's ability to make a choice between competing insurance carriers. Not that choosing between health plans is easy; indeed, it may be complex, but this problem can be overcome. Consider the United States' Federal Employees' Health Benefits Program, introduced in 1960, which now covers several million people. The American government pays each of its employees a fixed sum which can be used to buy health insurance from over 20 competing insurers. The subsidy is about 75 per cent of the total cost, and so if employees choose a cheaper plan they make a personal saving. Comparing different insurance plans is difficult and certainly surveying every insurer in the market would be very time-consuming. To reduce the time it would take to compare alternatives, the options have been put in simple tabular form in a cheap booklet published annually by a non-profit Washington consumer organisation. It gives the consumer a common measure of each insurance plan, a kind of annual percentage rate of insurance policies, regardless of the small print.[1]

This example underlines the general message that there is a useful role for consumer organisations in publishing information which assists consumers to make informed choices, not only among competing insurers, but also between providers. *Which?* supplies information on marketed products to some 600,000 subscribers. Perhaps in the future we may see a *Where?* magazine recommending the best hospitals or a *Who?* magazine advising patients on the best doctors. The publication of surgical mortality comparisons by the Health Care Financing Administration also suggests that government can play a useful role, and in the early stages of any transition to a competitive market its role in informing consumers may have to be substantial, not least because it alone has the power to compel a secretive medical profession to disclose the information consumers require to avoid falling into unsafe hands. There is also a vital role for organised groups of consumers to counteract the power of providers and insurers.

To sum up: there is a danger that doctors will exploit patients, not least by recommending 'unnecessary' treatment. It is said that doctors can exploit patients because doctors

---

[1] W. Francis, *Checkbook's Guide to Health Insurance Plans for Federal Employees* (1985).

have better knowledge about whether or not a given treatment will improve their health status. In reality, the doctor can take advantage of the patient because frequently no one can be sure what the outcome of a given medical intervention will be. As Professor Arrow appears to have understood, the threat of exploitation is the result of the uncertainty facing *all* parties, not merely the relative ignorance of the consumer, though that is also an important factor. We should therefore be sceptical of institutions which have developed and commanded support on the ground that the profession can be trusted to protect patients from exploitation. Professionalism does assist consumers in some ways but the price of professional self-regulation has been the imposition of restrictive practices which serve the pecuniary interests of doctors and protect bad performers from scrutiny. Professionalism and present regulatory arrangements are man-made institutions and we should ask whether better methods of protecting consumers can be discovered. And, at the minimum, we should not put obstacles in the path of new institutions or remedies which truly help consumers to avoid exploitation.

3

INSURANCE AND COST-EFFECTIVENESS: US EVIDENCE

INSURANCE, whether private or social, has been the response in most countries to uncertainty about the incidence of ill-health. In Britain the government tries to finance health care from taxation and I have suggested that the resulting problems should lead us to consider a bigger role for alternative sources of finance, including private insurance.

Professor Arrow identified three 'significant practical limits on the use of insurance', moral hazard, adverse selection and economies of scale.[1] This chapter deals with the problem of moral hazard. Adverse selection and economies of scale are considered in Chapter 6 when I discuss the rules necessary to make insurance markets serve the interests of all.

Moral Hazard

The problem of 'moral hazard' is succinctly described by Gordon McLachlan and Professor Alan Maynard: third-party payment (whether by insurance companies or anonymous taxpayers) 'reduces the price barriers to consumption and provides incentives for patients to over-consume' so that there are 'few incentives for decision-makers to . . . ensure costs are minimised and benefit maximised'.[2]

Does American evidence support the view that moral hazard is an unavoidable feature of health insurance? Until the mid-1970s the cost-containment record of American insurance companies was poor, but in America today, cost-containment

---

[1] Arrow, *op. cit.*, p. 961.
[2] McLachlan and Maynard (1982), p. 554.

is increasingly the norm. The lead has been taken by employers who, because of the cost of their employees' health plans, were finding it difficult to stay in business. In 1984 Chrysler, for instance, had to sell 70,000 vehicles just to pay for its employees' health benefits. In this paper the chief developments are summarised; a fuller account can be found in *Challenge to the NHS*.[1]

The methods used by insurers to limit spending can be placed in three groups. First, insurers put providers under financial constraints. Health maintenance organisations (HMOs) (to which subscribers pay a fixed monthly premium in return for all 'necessary' health-care services without any further obligation to pay fees) use financial incentives to encourage doctors to be cost-effective; and preferred provider organisations (PPOs) reduce costs by encouraging the use of approved (preferred) hospitals, believed to be more efficient. Second, insurers share costs with patients, who might pay all bills up to a fixed sum before cover begins (similar to the car insurance excess) or pay perhaps 20 per cent of each doctor's bill. Third, insurers apply checks and balances to clinical decisions, for instance, by employing 'nurse reviewers' to ensure that doctors do not hospitalise patients for too long.

1. Putting Financial Pressure on Doctors

Health Maintenance Organisations: Until recently the growth of HMOs was stifled by a hostile medical profession. The number began to increase during the 1970s though it was not until 1982 that the Supreme Court declared AMA boycotts of HMOs to be unlawful.[2] Now there is at least one in every major metropolitan area. In 1972 there were 142 HMOs with 5.3 million members, but by June 1985 membership had increased to 19 million and the number of HMOs had risen to nearly 400.[3] Between June 1985 and June 1986, membership increased by a further 25 per cent to 24 million, while the number of HMOs rose to almost 600.[4] By March 1987 the total membership had risen to nearly 28 million in 650 HMOs.[5]

---

[1] Green (1986).
[2] 452 US 969 (1982).
[3] Interstudy (1985a).
[4] Interstudy (1986).
[5] *Interstudy Edge*, Summer 1987, p. 1.

There are four main types of HMO — the staff, group, network and independent practice association (IPA) models — though there are many hybrids. In the staff HMO, doctors are usually salaried employees who provide care at a central location under the control of the HMO. Under the group model, the HMO contracts with an independent, often preexisting, group practice at a single location. The physicians, both generalists and specialists, receive a capitation payment, usually paid monthly. The network model is like the group model except that the HMO contracts with more than one independent group practice. The IPA is an arrangement whereby the HMO contracts with a variety of doctors, most of whom are in solo practice, but some of whom may be in groups. They are usually paid by the HMO on a fee-for-service basis.

IPAs have been growing most rapidly, chiefly because they combine some of the advantages of traditional fee-for-service medicine with the cost restraint of other types of HMO. In June 1986 they comprised 58 per cent of all HMOs, with staff models 12 per cent, group 14 per cent and network 16 per cent. Traditionally, HMOs were non-profit but recently, largely in an effort to raise capital for expansion from the equity market, more have become for-profit. In March 1987, 64 per cent were for-profit, up from 18 per cent in 1981, though not-for-profit plans accounted for 56 per cent of all members.[1]

In the past, HMOs were typically local community health plans. Now there are over 20 national firms with HMOs in more than one state, 10 of which opened for business between June 1984 and June 1985. In 1985 the top seven HMO firms (Kaiser, CIGNA, Health America, Maxicare, US Health Care Systems, Prudential and United) accounted for over 80 per cent of total national HMO firm membership and 44 per cent of all HMO membership.[2]

HMOs depend for their success on being able to offer comprehensive services at a competitive price. They use a range of strategies, including financial incentives to doctors not to over-use hospital facilities, informal peer pressure, utilisation review including pre-admission certification and concurrent

---

[1] *Interstudy Edge*, Summer 1987, p. 7.
[2] Interstudy (1985b).

review, lifestyle and 'wellness' education programmes for members, preventive health programmes, and searching out cost-effective providers.

The economic significance of HMOs is that, because they threaten the position of established suppliers, they increase the bargaining power of the consumer and discipline the monopoly power of organised medicine. In a study for the Federal Trade Commission, Goldberg and Greenberg found that the presence of an HMO produced an increase in Blue Cross benefits, reduced bed utilisation rates for members of Blue Cross as well as other organisations, and induced the Blues to found their own HMOs.[1]

The HMO selects only those physicians who come up to scratch. Staff, group and network HMOs pay their doctors either a salary or a capitation fee, so that the financial incentive to over-hospitalise is removed. Under the IPA model doctors do have an incentive to over-use hospitals, but this is checked by utilisation review procedures. IPA doctors also face financial incentives. Physician Care of Washington, DC, for instance, has a fixed-fee schedule of 85 per cent of usual, customary and reasonable fees. Initially, 20 per cent of this fee is withheld, and at the end of the year each doctor's utilisation record is examined. Doctors judged to have over-used services may receive only a proportion of the withheld sum.

Thus, instead of paying individual doctors' fees or hospital bills, the consumer pays a fixed monthly sum in return for comprehensive care from a set of known providers acting in an environment designed to promote cost-effective treatment. The HMO also reduces the moral hazard by eliminating the third party and acting as both provider and insurer.

Incentive for Under-provision

The chief disadvantage of HMOs is that they have an incentive to *under*-provide medical services. A recent study in Seattle contrasts the health status of three groups of patients: (a) members of a local HMO; (b) fee-for-service patients required to share costs through co-payments or deductibles; and (c) fee-for-service patients with no cost-sharing. The study found

---

[1] Goldberg and Greenberg (1977), pp. 110-18.

that for most people HMO care saved money and may have contributed to better health. But low-income participants who joined the experiment with health problems were in some ways in worse health at the end of the five-year study. The authors were uncertain about the reasons for this difference, but the HMO itself recognised that poor members were more likely to suffer from under-treatment and had introduced an 'outreach' programme of medical services for poor families to remedy this weakness.[1] However, other studies have found no difference between the treatment of HMO and fee-for-service patients.[2] Several HMOs have erected internal safeguards against under-provision, but the subscriber's chief protection is his ability to take his money elsewhere. It is vital to maintain the consumer's freedom to choose, so that HMOs can flourish only by satisfying their customers.

Preferred Provider Organisations: The recent rapid growth of preferred provider organisations (PPOs) has been a competitive reaction to the expansion of HMOs. An individual who joins an HMO pays a fixed monthly premium and the HMO is at financial risk for any health care which is required by the subscriber and included in the contract. Above all, the HMO 'locks-in' its subscribers, that is, if they go to a doctor outside the HMO panel they have no insurance cover. This is not always popular and the PPO overcomes it by allowing people a wider choice. If consumers choose to use the services of a doctor on the PPO's approved panel they are of course covered, but if they use an outside hospital or doctor they still enjoy cover, though at a lower rate of 80 per cent or less. Thus, the individual with a serious illness who decides to take no chances and opts to consult a specialist of high repute who is not on the PPO's panel can do so and still enjoy insurance cover. Significantly, a few HMOs have reacted to the growth of PPOs by introducing a new model, an 'open-ended' HMO. Generally, this combines HMO cover with traditional indemnity insurance for doctors outside the panel, usually with significant co-payments or deductibles. Some 360,000 people had joined open-ended HMOs by March 1987.[3]

---

[1] Ware *et al.* (1986).

[2] E.g., Yelin *et al.* (1985).

[3] *Interstudy Edge*, Summer 1987, pp. 2-3.

For the doctor or hospital the attraction of a PPO is the opportunity to increase market share. In addition, neither doctor nor hospital bears a financial risk. They are paid agreed discounted fees by directly billing the insurer, thus avoiding bad debts and the costly necessity to bill patients individually. For the insurer and purchaser (employer) the attraction of the PPO is that it is a halfway house between an HMO and traditional fee-for-service. It is a simple way for insurers or purchasers to identify cost-effective providers and it is easier to establish than an HMO, needing only an agreement about fee levels, utilisation review, and the details of claiming and billing. There is no capital expenditure.

The rise of PPOs has been rapid. In 1975 there were none. In 1982 the American Hospital Association identified 33 in its first survey and by December 1984 it had found 115.[1] At the end of 1986 the American Medical Care Review Association put the number of PPOs at 454, with an estimated 30 million members, while a further 52 organisations were at the development stage.[2] At least a quarter of hospitals and physicians now have PPO contracts.

Thus, in a total American population of about 250 million, there are some 58 million people in either HMOs or PPOs, a tenfold increase since the mid-1970s.

2. Cost-Sharing

Employers have attempted to share costs with employees in the hope of reducing the incentive to choose the most expensive care. Cost-sharing includes co-insurance, whereby the employee pays a proportion of all bills, usually 20 per cent; or co-payments, a term generally reserved for fixed subscriber contributions (e.g. $5 for each visit to a doctor) as opposed to percentage payments. Deductibles have also been increased, because 'first-dollar' coverage of small and regular expenditures is costly to administer. The deductible is the amount which must be paid by an insured person before insurance cover begins, like the 'excess' in motor insurance. It is often an annual figure of about $200. In 1980 only 5 per cent of health

---

[1] *Hospitals*, 1 September 1985, pp. 68-73.
[2] AMCRA (1985; and 1986 update).

plans required a deductible of $100 or more, whereas by 1985 43 per cent did so.[1]

Several companies have introduced flexible benefits packages in which employees choose between health plans at varying costs. If they choose a cheaper one, they can share in the savings. The oldest example of a multiple-choice plan is the Federal Employees Health Benefits Plan introduced in 1960 to cover employees of the Federal Government. Employees receive a fixed dollar subsidy and may choose from among a number of registered alternatives. Many private companies also offer multiple-choice schemes. In 1984, for instance, General Motors introduced its Informed Choice Plan under which employees can choose between HMOs, a PPO and managed fee-for-service options.[2]

In a few cases companies have introduced 'cafeteria' plans, offering an array of tax-deductible benefits like pensions as well as health care. Savings made from one plan may be spent on another benefit, though not taken as cash. The chief advantage for the employer is that in each contract cycle he can agree to contribute a fixed cash sum, whereas in the past employers often agreed to supply a prescribed set of health benefits and then had to go out and buy the previously agreed package in an uncompetitive market. The employee gains flexibility. If he chooses to invest more in a pension than in a health plan, he can do so. This is especially helpful to the growing number of families with two wage-earners. Instead of being in two health plans, one partner can gain family health cover at his workplace, and the other can invest in a pension or other benefit at hers.

3. Checks and Balances on Clinical Decisions

Not only have HMO doctors accepted financial discipline; they have also accepted limits on their style of practice and submitted to quality assurance checks. An HMO will usually have a medical director who will set standards for his staff and question them if their approach deviates from the accepted pattern. A great many studies have shown significant variations in the use of health-care services across geographic areas

---

[1] Gabel *et al.* (1987), p. 47.
[2] *Business and Health,* September 1987, pp. 28-9.

and sometimes these differences have been explained as the result of the number of physicians, or hospital beds, or the age composition of the population. But a recent study by the Rand Corporation set out to discover whether differences resulted from 'inappropriate use'. They examined the application of three procedures applied to the Medicare population in 1981, coronary angiography, carotid endarterectomy, and upper gastrointestinal tract endoscopy. Across all sites studied they found 'inappropriate use' of coronary angiography in 17 per cent of cases, of carotid endarterectomy in 32 per cent, and of upper gastrointestinal tract endoscopy in 17 per cent.[1] As concern about 'inappropriate care' has grown, so insurance companies have become increasingly anxious to identify and eliminate it. Second opinions for surgery are now common, as well as pre-admission review, during which the insurance company tries to settle the cost of treatment before it begins, so that subscribers know where they stand and doctors cannot charge whatever they please.

Some of the 'managed-care' techniques, and particularly pre-admission review, developed by HMOs to limit 'inappropriate use' and control costs are now being used by fee-for-service insurers as they fight to remain competitive. In 1982 only 2 per cent of the business of commercial insurers (that is, not including Blue Cross/Blue Shield) took the form of managed care. In 1984 the figure was still only 4 per cent, but by 1986 it was 29 per cent and rising. Sometimes this has taken the form of establishing HMOs and PPOs, but in three-quarters of cases companies have applied managed-care techniques to fee-for-service insurance.[2]

Second Surgical Opinions: Second opinions for surgery have been made mandatory by many insurers including Blue Cross, the once-dominant non-profit insurer. They often produce non-confirmation rates of between 25 and 30 per cent. Usually the insurer pays for second and even third opinions, but Blue Cross subscribers who fail to comply must pay the first $1,000 of the hospital bill and all the surgeon's and anaesthetist's charges. Otherwise the insurer pays in full. Second opinions

---

[1] Chassin *et al.* (1987), pp. 2,533-47.
[2] Gabel *et al., op. cit.*, pp. 46-60.

can produce reductions in surgery, though there is now controversy over the extent of real savings.

Pre-admission Approval: Increasingly, insurers are requiring patients to obtain pre-admission approval before entering hospital (except in emergencies). After seeing their doctor the patient must telephone the insurance company to obtain its agreement to enter hospital. The call will be taken by a trained nurse with several years of clinical experience who will decide whether a hospital stay is justified. If appropriate, the cheaper alternative of one-day surgery will be suggested, or, if hospital care is justified, the 'nurse reviewer' will decide how many days the patient can spend in hospital. Unnecessary days in hospital are very costly and many insurers, for instance, are currently trying to prevent the common practice of admitting patients to hospital on the night before an operation, a practice they regard as medically unnecessary. A measure of counselling also occurs as nurse reviewers speak to patients. If need be, the nurse will telephone the doctor to ensure that everyone sees eye to eye. The nurse reviewer also tries to schedule surgery on the day of admission, and to co-ordinate laboratory tests and X-rays in advance.

Concurrent Review: During hospitalisation there is concurrent review, to double-check the necessity for diagnostic and surgical procedures carried out in hospital and to avoid unnecessarily long stays. Discharge planning is also a common feature of managed care. Nurse reviewers, sometimes by going on-site, ensure that physicians do not allow patients to remain in hospital any longer than required, and make arrangements for home care backed by specialist nursing support or other alternatives. This is not only a matter of saving money; by avoiding unnecessary days in hospital patients can increase their chances of escaping the virulent infections which are often found there.

Utilisation Review: Often, utilisation review takes the form of 'profile analysis' of providers, during which the hospitalisation record of individual doctors is contrasted with the average or the median. The main objective is to identify the rogue providers, or 'outliers', and to modify their behaviour.

Within preferred provider groups such information can be used to terminate the participation of unsatisfactory doctors, and employers are becoming increasingly sophisticated in steering people away from high-cost, low-quality providers.

All told, these methods mean that doctors cannot order any treatment they like regardless of cost. The scope for doctors to inflate demand has, therefore, been substantially curtailed.

Why was Cost-Containment Slow to Emerge?

Employers, through whom most Americans are insured, have been the driving force behind these developments. After years of paying bills without much question companies now aim to be 'smart buyers':

> 'Smart buyers are companies that simultaneously seek out the best price for health care while also preserving standards of efficiency, quality and access. Buying cheap is not buying smart.'[1]

But an important question remains. For many years health insurers in America did not promote cost-effectiveness. Why did they tolerate ever-rising costs for so long? There were two main factors.

As the earlier IEA study, *Challenge to the NHS*, revealed, the AMA applied sanctions to insurers who tried to contain costs and we know that this practice has persisted until recently. The insurance industry was well developed in the early years of the century in states like Washington and Oregon. Doctors were warned about unnecessary surgery, asked to justify hospitalisation and had their bills checked. Insurers in Oregon, for instance, usually insisted that no patient be admitted to hospital without the advance approval of the insurer. But in the 1940s the doctors boycotted the insurance companies and set up their own. The boycott turned patients against the traditional insurers and they switched to the doctor-controlled insurance company. Faced with either going out of business or toeing the doctors' line, they chose the latter, abandoning attempts to control unnecessary surgery by second opinions and scrutinising doctors' bills.

---

[1] Bachman *et al.* (1987), p. 28.

Such boycotts occurred until very recently, but when the Federal Trade Commission intervened from the mid-1970s to outlaw the restrictions imposed on insurers by the AMA, the insurance industry began to compete.

The second reason for rising costs was the third-party status of the insurer. Until the mid-1970s the vast majority of Americans who had private insurance were covered through their employer's tax-subsidised health plan which usually arranged comprehensive health benefits through an outside insurance company. From the individual's point of view, there was not one anonymous payer, but two. One was the employer, who probably paid the whole of the premium and who in a competitive labour market did not want to upset his workers by penny-pinching and, because of the open-ended tax subsidy, was less conscious of health costs than other business expenses. The other was the insurer, who sold insurance cover to the employer. This divided responsibility created an especially strong incentive for individual employees to consume health-care services with total disregard for the cost.

This problem remains, but integration of insurance and provision is helping to overcome it. The most significant response has come from HMOs and PPOs, which have abandoned the traditional third-party payment role by integrating health-care delivery with insurance. Self-insurance has also been growing. This means that companies hold their own premiums and pay their own claims, often through a third-party administrator whose *raison d'être* is the avoidance of waste. In 1977, 16 per cent of insurance premiums were paid by companies wholly or partly self-insured. By 1986 the figure had increased to 36 per cent.[1]

Price Competition or Quality Competition?

That there has been a re-awakening of competition in American health care in the last few years is not disputed, but it has not taken the form of price competition alone. Using 1982 data for 5,732 US hospitals, Robinson and Luft found that hospitals with many local rivals engaged in a competitive

---

[1] *Health Care Financing Review*, Summer 1987, Table 21.

struggle which led to increases in average costs per admission and that average costs were higher in those areas where hospitals faced more rivals. In markets with more than 10 hospitals within a 24-kilometre radius, average costs per admission were 26 per cent higher than in hospitals with no competitors within a similar radius, and average costs per patient-day were 15 per cent higher. This was because hospitals also compete, not only on price, but also in terms of the perceived quality of care and the level of amenities offered. Where patients make the key choice of location, as in maternity cases, hospitals compete by offering a range of 'alternative' delivery methods, pre-natal classes for the expectant parents in everything from delivery technique to the avoidance of sibling rivalry, and by providing a 'homely' atmosphere. Where the patient relies heavily on advice from a doctor, hospitals have sought to make themselves attractive to doctors by offering benefits like convenient parking, office space and clerical support, as well as the most up-to-date technology and a good nurse-to-bed ratio: 'I wouldn't say that competition wasn't operating', said Luft. 'It was a very competitive environment; it just wasn't price competition'.[1] Until 1982 or 1983, he explained, 'Price didn't matter in the hospital industry, so competition occurred in a different way — on the basis of quality of service'.[2] Hospital competition in these respects has certainly increased consumer satisfaction, but it has not necessarily improved clinical outcomes for patients.

Robinson and Luft's study covered the period before cost-containment efforts began to bite from about 1983 onwards. They are borne out by a second study conducted by Catherine McLaughlin, who examined the impact on price competition of HMOs. It was once argued that HMOs would compel rivals to lower prices, but McLaughlin found that in areas of high HMO penetration there were fewer admissions to hospitals and lower lengths of stay, but higher hospital expenses per day and per admission. This is partly because less serious cases are treated outside the hospital setting, thus leaving more serious cases requiring more intensive treatment, but also because

---

[1] Robinson and Luft (1987), pp. 3,241-45.
[2] *Hospitals*, 20 December 1987, pp. 34-5.

the competitive reaction of rivals has not necessarily been to cut prices; rather they have sought to convince consumers that they offer a higher quality service.[1]

Both these studies, as their authors recognise, predate the post-1983 growth of cost-containment. Has the new atmosphere produced more price competition? According to Robinson and Luft, price competition resulting from hospitals contracting with HMOs, PPOs, and Medicaid programmes 'can be expected to reduce costs', though non-price competition is likely to remain. The continued importance of non-price competition, they thought, would help to prevent cost-containment efforts leading to reductions in quality.[2] Studies of California, where hospital contracting has grown rapidly, bear out this claim.

A survey of the responses of Californian doctors to PPOs in 1986 suggests that price competition has been growing. Early PPOs tried to contain costs by negotiating discounts from usual, customary and reasonable fees, but later they switched increasingly to fixed-fee schedules. Over 80 per cent of doctors surveyed reported that their fees had been reduced by 10 per cent, nearly a quarter by between 20 and 30 per cent, and 15 per cent had reduced fees by over 30 per cent.[3]

But price discounting is not the only concern of employers, the chief purchasers of health insurance. The first generation of PPOs laid heavy stress on discounts in return for volume. Between 1983 and 1985 many Californian hospitals, for instance, gave discounts of 17-25 per cent but did not increase their throughput by as much as they anticipated. Subsequently, PPO contracts have laid more emphasis on quality, through systematic peer review, risk-adjusted outcome indices, laying down treatment standards and appropriate-care protocols. Above all, medical outcomes are being monitored to discover whether patients regained optimal functioning after treatment.[4]

---

[1] McLaughlin (1987), pp. 183-205.
[2] Robinson and Luft (1987), p. 3,244.
[3] Johns and Jones (1987), pp. 59-69.
[4] Boland (1987), pp. 75-81.

The Impact on Hospital Use

About 40 per cent of US health spending comes from government sources, largely Medicare (the federal scheme for the elderly and disabled) and Medicaid (the joint federal/state programme for the poor), where cost containment has also been the order of the day. The new climate of cost containment in both public and private sectors has brought about a fall in hospital use. There are about 6,800 hospitals in the USA with around 1.3 million beds, mostly classified as 'community hospitals'. The number of hospital in-patient admissions fell by 6 per cent between 1984 and 1985, having fallen by 10 per cent from the 1981 peak figure.[1] The average length of patient stay in non-federal short-stay hospitals fell between 1979 and 1984 from 7.2 to 6.6 days, though it has subsequently increased slightly, reflecting the greater severity of condition of remaining in-patients as less serious cases have obtained care in out-patient settings. The number of days spent in hospital per 1,000 population has fallen from 1,111 in 1979 to around 970 patient-days per 1,000 population in 1985.[2] Day surgery in America accounts for about 50 per cent of all surgical cases, whereas in the UK the comparable figure is more like 20 per cent. Hospital occupancy rates have also been falling. In 1980 the hospital occupancy rate for 'community hospitals' was 75.2 per cent; by 1984 the rate was 69.3 per cent and falling. After many years during which the number of hospital beds increased, the total began to fall in 1984.[3]

These trends are in part the result of a shift to increased use of more cost-effective out-patient facilities. Out-patient visits rose by 10 per cent from 220.9 million in 1981 to 243.4 million in 1985.[4] The pattern of employment in the health-care industry has also changed as a result of cost-containment. In 1976 hospital employment accounted for about 66 per cent of all health service employment, while in 1986 the figure had fallen to 55 per cent.[5]

---

[1] *Health United States*, 1986, Table 63.
[2] *Health United States*, 1986, Tables 59-60; *Hospitals*, 5 October 1986, p.68.
[3] *Health United States*, 1986, Tables 79, 83.
[4] *Hospitals*, 5 October 1986, p. 67.
[5] *Health Care Financing Review*, Summer 1987, p. 1.

The Impact on Spending and Average Prices

The individual companies which have been in the forefront of efforts to contain costs have made very substantial savings. The car manufacturer Chrysler, for instance, anticipated in 1983 that unless it acted decisively its company health plan would cost over $460 million in 1984. By re-designing its health plan, eliminating waste and educating its employees, Chrysler limited spending to $402 million, a $58 million reduction.[1] However despite the success of individual companies and notwithstanding the widespread improvements in the cost-effectiveness of medical treatment, total expenditure on health care in America has not been falling. It continues to increase in absolute terms and as a proportion of GNP, rising from 9.4 per cent in 1981 to 10.5 per cent in 1983, slipping back in 1984 to 10.3 per cent, but rising in 1985 to 10.6 per cent and nudging 11 per cent in 1986.[2]

According to the AMA, as a direct result of increasing competition, the real purchasing power of doctors' incomes fell during 1984. The median physician's net income after expenses but before taxes increased by 2 per cent between 1983 and 1984, less than the rate of inflation.[3] And in 1985 net earnings fell in real terms by the largest margin since *Medical Economics* began its regular authoritative survey. In 1986, however, net earnings rose by 10 per cent, the biggest percentage increase since 1979. These sharp changes mask the long-run trend revealed by the figures for the decade 1975-1985. Taking inflation into account, the median net income of physicians fell by 5 per cent.[4] Competitive pressure has also made a very big difference to newcomers to the profession. They have often had to embark on their careers as salaried employees at relatively low incomes rather than as self-employed solo practitioners. Perhaps the main effect of competition on doctors has been that they have had to submit to increased scrutiny of their activities in the form of utilisa-

---

[1] Califano (1986), p. 25.
[2] *Health United States*, 1986, Table 89; *US Industrial Outlook*, 1987, 54-1; *Health Care Financing Review*, Summer 1987, Table 12.
[3] AMA (1985), pp. 1, 8-9.
[4] Clare, Spratly, Schwab, and Iglehart (1987), pp. 101-2.

tion review or quality assurance systems operated by both hospitals and insurers.

The consumer price index (CPI) for medical care items did not increase as fast between 1982 and 1985 as it had in previous years. During the five-year period 1975-80 the average annual increase was 9.5 per cent, and in 1979-80, 1980-81 and 1981-82 the increases were 10.9, 10.8 and 11.6 per cent respectively. In 1982-83 the increase slowed to 8.7 per cent, and in both 1983-84 and 1984-85 it was lower still at 6.2 per cent. However, the average price level of medical goods increased faster than for goods generally. The CPI for all items in 1984-85 rose by 3.6 per cent, and for all services by 5.1 per cent.[1]

The high level of spending in the USA as a proportion of GNP compared with Britain is explained partly by the higher quality of service provided in America. This has much to do with a higher standard of amenities which may make little or no difference to outcomes, but there are also some indications that higher spending produces a better quality outcome for patients. America spends 2.8 times more per head than Britain and 1.7 times more than the French. Differences in life expectancy are not large, but the nosocomial (post-operative) infection rate in the USA at 4 per cent is much lower than France's 7 per cent and Britain's 10 per cent.[2]

Some particular factors also explain recent increases in American spending. Possibly the single most important is the huge open-ended government tax subsidy to employer health plans, estimated in 1986 to be worth about $49 billion when total spending was $458 billion.[3] There has also been continuous pressure from rising malpractice insurance premiums and the growing number of elderly persons using expensive services. A larger number, for instance, are now reliant on nursing homes. In 1982, there were some 14,500 nursing homes (with 25 beds or more) providing in all about 1.5 million beds. The cost of nursing-home care, just under half of which is paid for by Medicare and Medicaid (mainly

[1] *Health United States*, 1986, Tables 86, 88.
[2] Schieber and Poullier (1987), p. 112.
[3] Enthoven (1985), p. 3; *Health Care Financing Review*, Summer 1987, Table 13.

the latter), is rising faster than the average for all health-care items, 10.6 per cent in 1984-85 compared with the average of 8.9 per cent.[1] Spending on long-term care by Medicaid was about $13 billion in 1986.[2]

Expenditure on home-health care is also growing rapidly. It is not easy to calculate, but one US government estimate puts spending in 1985 at over $2 billion. Medicare re-imbursement for home-health care alone reached $1.6 billion, up from $519 million in 1978.[3]

To sum up: the climate of cost containment in the USA has produced dramatic changes in hospital use. In-patient days, for instance, are at an 18-year low. Total spending, however, continues to rise in real terms, partly because of price rises, which reflect higher quality as well as rising labour costs, and partly because new demands are being made, especially for nursing-home places and home-nursing care. It is also because a continued open-ended tax subsidy conceals the true cost, and, not least, because many Americans want to spend at a high level on health care, as the high level of out-of-pocket spending testifies. Nearly 29 per cent of American personal health expenditure still comes from direct out-of-pocket payment.[4]

In conclusion: the most serious criticism of health insurance is that it is inherently incapable of containing costs, and until the mid-1970s this was a valid complaint about American health insurers. But this weakness had much to do with the restrictive practices enforced by the mighty American Medical Association, which in recent years has had its wings clipped by the Federal Trade Commission. Subsequently there has been a renewal of competition, and now the promotion of cost-effectiveness is the order of the day.

---

[1] *Health United States*, 1986, Tables 85, 95.
[2] *Modern Health Care*, 16 January 1987, p. 42.
[3] *US Industrial Outlook*, 1987, p. 54-4.
[4] *Health Care Financing Review*, Summer 1987, Table 15.

NATIONAL INSURANCE AND COST-EFFECTIVENESS: EVIDENCE FROM EUROPE

Responsiveness to Demand

Most European countries have some form of compulsory health insurance scheme. They have generally proved better able to reflect consumer demand than arrangements which rely on an annual government budget allocation financed from taxation. In this chapter I will examine briefly the Belgian, French and German systems. First I consider Belgium, because it comes closest to Britain in GNP per head. Why is Belgian spending higher?

Belgium: It has a compulsory national insurance scheme covering practically the whole population. There are about 1,700 sick funds providing health insurance, divided into six groups. Compulsory insurance contributions, paid by employers and employees, go first to the National Social Security Office and then to the National Institute for Sickness and Invalidity Insurance, which divides them among the six groups.

Patients pay GPs a standard fee and claim re-imbursement from their chosen sick fund. Normally they receive 75 per cent, but special categories, such as the disabled, pensioners and widows receive a full refund. Doctors are free to prescribe any medicines, but patients are re-imbursed at four different rates. 'Life-saving' drugs are fully refunded, but patients must pay 25 per cent of the cost of 'therapeutically-useful' medications, up to an agreed maximum (special category patients pay only 15 per cent, up to a lower maximum). For 'less-useful' medicines patients must pay 50 per cent, up to a maximum. Pharmacists are paid the balance by the sick funds. Other drugs are not re-imburseable.

Hospital patients must pay a daily fee, fixed by law, to cover hotel and nursing costs and are billed separately for doctors' services and drugs. Sick funds will refund the hospital charge for the first 40 days in hospital, but no more. The services of hospital doctors and drugs are re-imbursed on the same basis as for GPs. In addition, the government pays 95 per cent of the cost of treating an approved list of conditions like cancer, tuberculosis, poliomyelitis, mental illness and mental handicap.

Belgium differs from Britain in two main respects. First, most funding comes from national insurance rather than taxation, and second, patients make significant out-of-pocket paymets. National insurance schemes are really systems of earmarked taxation, but they differ from straight tax-funded systems like the NHS in that the consumer has an explicit contract with the sick fund. Thus, if a doctor considers that a patient would benefit from a particular treatment it must be provided; whilst in Britain, patients may be acknowledged to be in need of treatment which is nonetheless withheld due to politically determined budgetary constraint. The British government fixes an annual budget allocation for hospital and community services and requires district health authorities to function within this limit. Compulsory national insurance schemes put no such political constraints on total spending.

Between 1977 and 1984 Britain devoted a smaller share of GNP to health than other developed nations, annually about 25 per cent less than the average. And Britain's low spending makes a huge difference. If we had spent at the level of Belgium, the country closest to Britain in national output, we would have expended £49 more per head, in total about £2.8 billion more at 1984 prices.

Controlling Costs

The other characteristic of national insurance schemes is the deep involvement of governments in fixing medical fees and hospital re-imbursement rates.

West Germany: Over 90 per cent of Germans belong to a

statutory health insurance scheme covering hospital and primary care, whilst a further 8 per cent are covered by private insurance. About 7 per cent of people in the state scheme also have additional private insurance. Doctors and hospitals are paid by non-profit sickness funds, of which there are some 1,400 divided into eight categories. They are required by law to pay not only for primary and hospital care but also sick pay, and a long list of other services. Each fund charges its own premium, varying from 7 to 14 per cent (12 per cent on average) of earnings, which is then deducted from pay packets, with the cost split fifty-fifty between employer and employee.

The main worry in Germany is that costs have risen out of control. There are two main reasons, neither an inherent defect of insurance as such. First, the tradition of German health insurance has been that services should be free at the time of use, an attitude which, as under the NHS, has encouraged waste and over-utilisation typified by the right of patients who have undergone surgery to a period of recuperation in a spa town.

Second, German governments over many years have chosen to contain spending by government price regulation instead of by encouraging price competition. These efforts have been unsuccessful, chiefly because of the corporatist nature of German government which allows doctors to exercise undue influence on the price-fixing machinery.

Doctors' fees are not paid directly by patients who then claim from their insurer, but each quarter sickness funds give subscribers a certificate which they show to doctors to obtain treatment without further charge. The sickness funds do not pay doctors direct; instead they pay local associations of doctors who pass on the fees to individual members. Membership of these associations (Kassenärztliche Vereinigungen or 'KVs'), of which there are 18, is compulsory. As well as paying doctors, they are responsible for seeing that patients receive their statutory entitlement to 'adequate, effective, and economically sound' medical attention. This method of payment has re-inforced the ability of the organised medical profession to impede competition and raise prices. Moreover, from the mid-1960s KVs began to be paid by the sickness funds on a fee-for-service basis instead of by capitation payments, though the KVs had always disbursed payments to their members by the former method. This switch to fee-for-service significantly fuelled German cost escalation.

The hospital service is separate and hospital doctors are not allowed to treat patients outside the hospital setting. Roughly equal numbers of German doctors work in hospitals and in private practice. Unlike Britain, about half the specialists in West Germany work in private practice and around 40 per cent in the hospitals. Also unlike Britain, patients can go directly to specialists in private practice without referral by a GP. If hospital treatment is necessary a doctor in private practice must transfer the patient to the care of a hospital. This sharp division is also found in the NHS and is regarded by German analysts as one of the weaknesses of their system. Just over half the hospital beds are in public hospitals, about a third in private non-profit voluntary hospitals, frequently run by churches, and 12 per cent are in for-profit hospitals, usually owned by doctors. Since 1972 hospitals have been paid according to their allowable costs and re-imbursed fully for their services so long as they are judged to be operating effectively and economically, a method which has proved inflationary because hospitals have an incentive to keep patients in for longer than medically necessary in order to increase their revenue. Thus, using OECD figures, the average length of stay in German hospitals in 1980 was 18.4 days compared with the average for the seven leading OECD nations of 13.1. The French figure was 13.5, the UK 13.3 and the USA 7.3.[1]

The current costs of hospitals are separated from their investment costs. The former are charged to the sickness funds while investment costs are paid by federal, state, or local government from taxes. Sick funds are charged a daily rate, fixed ultimately by government, but negotiated initially between regional groups of hospitals before being submitted to provincial governments for approval. The sickness funds are also organised into provincial associations for negotiating purposes. Additional services (single room, TV, telephone, extra food, choice of doctor) are paid for by patients. Most hospital doctors are salaried, though heads of clinical depart-

[1] OECD (1987), Table 32.

ments often add substantially to their earnings by treating patients privately.

Over the last few years German governments have attempted to limit spending on health care. In 1977 a limit was placed on sickness fund premiums by linking rises to real incomes. An *'ad hoc'* parliament was established representing all interested groups and meets twice a year to agree fees. Some cost-sharing was introduced. In 1981 further cost-containment laws followed. Some fees were reduced, drug re-imbursement limited, and cost-sharing increased in small ways. The hospital cost-containment law of 1981 gave government more control of the daily rate, and introduced greater hospital planning controls, and reviews of hospital efficiency. But the sick funds continue to be obliged to re-imburse hospitals for their economically justifiable costs.

To sum up: in Germany there is competition between providers conducted largely in terms of the quality of service, but there is little price competition between hospitals or insurers. HMOs, which from American experience have proved capable of generating price competition, cannot function in Germany because of a decision in 1960 under which the KVs are legally prevented from providing medical care via panels of 'approved' doctors. Price-fixing machinery has been dominated by providers, a tendency encouraged by the corporatist nature of German decision-making.

The advantages of the German system are that patients have a contractual right to treatment, unlike under the NHS, and that hospitals compete for patients, thus raising standards of service. But the system is marred by the absence of price competition and by the continued predominance of the 'everything-possible, free-at-the-time-of-use' ethic. Above all, high costs in Germany reflect inept and counter-productive efforts by governments to regulate prices.

France: As in Germany, the French social security system is funded by compulsory contributions deducted from pay packets, though employers pay a higher share, 12.6 per cent of incomes, as against the employees' 5.5 per cent.

Doctors' fees since 1960 have been approved annually by the government, though some doctors remain outside the system. About one-third of all doctors work in hospitals on a salary, one-third are in private practice, and one-third are part-private and part-salaried. Some salaried doctors work for health centres, which are run by trade unions, the Red Cross or mutual aid societies. They are disliked by organised medicine and re-imbursed on a fee-for-service basis at a lower rate than normal. Of the active physicians, slightly under half are GPs. Specialists work partly in hospital and partly in private clinics and can be consulted by patients without referral.

In France a patient visiting a doctor, whether GP or specialist, pays the fee and claims a refund from the *caisses,* which are run by boards representing employers and trade unions. Generally the *caisses* refund 70 per cent of the approved charge, subject to a maximum patient payment in a monthly or six-monthly period. About half the population takes out 'gap insurance' to cover the patient's fraction of the approved fee, a service offered by some 7,000 non-profit insurance funds called *mutuelles.* Some doctors charge above government rates, in which case the individual pays the difference, though private insurance is also available for these higher fees. Nearly 3 million people are classified as poor and they receive all care free of charge.

There are some 400,000 public hospital beds and 175,000 private, mainly run by non-profit bodies though a few are for-profit. Private hospitals, however, carry out over half the surgery. As well as being subject to limits on revenue spending, hospital construction and the purchase of new equipment like scanners has to be authorised by the ministry of health. Usually each region is given a quota.

Thirty listed diseases, plus any others considered severe or chronic, are treated without charge. Medically qualified government inspectors, of whom there are about 4,000, approve hospital cases for full re-imbursement and authorise long stays. Psychiatric and maternity care is also free. Recently, a small charge of 27 francs (£2.70) has been introduced for each day in hospital, although the poor continue to pay nothing at all.

Until 1984 hospitals were paid a standard rate for every day a patient was in hospital, thus giving hospitals an incentive to hospitalise patients for longer than necessary. In that year, however, global budgets were introduced and subsequently hospital stays have been falling, a trend already under way since the 1960s.

'Life-saving' drugs are free, but a second group has been subject to a 70 per cent charge. 'Comfort' medicines, like laxatives, are eligible for a still smaller refund; but outlays on drugs are also subject to monthly and six-monthly out-of-pocket limits.

The chief characteristic of the French system is the very high rate of cost-sharing compared with Germany and Britain. In Britain, any suggestion that government should pay less than the full cost of health care, or that people should be allowed to pay more if they wish, leads to outbursts against a two-tier system. But French arrangements are not politically controversial and are accepted by socialists and communists as much as by the other political parties. Nor is it true to say that the poor are in some sense locked into a second-class service. Cost-sharing between patients and insurance companies is often valued by economists as a deterrent, but in France, total spending on health care is very high, 9.1 per cent of GDP in 1984, second only to the USA and Sweden, and higher than the German figure of 8.1 per cent and the UK's 5.9 per cent.[1] French spending is especially high on over-the-counter drugs, which require no doctor's prescription, and which are paid for in full by patients.

The Cost of Administration

Closely linked to the claim that health insurance is inherently incapable of promoting cost-effectiveness, is the complaint that insurance schemes are more costly to administer than the NHS.

First, the true cost of the NHS is concealed because the full cost of obtaining tax revenues is not included in official government figures. This is quite apart from the hidden cost of reducing each person's disposable income and therefore their power to support alternatives capable of generating price competition. In addition, the NHS is under-managed in the sense that its costs are unknown and its quality of service is

---

[1] OECD (1987), p. 55.

not evaluated, and to remedy these fundamental deficiencies might well require additional staff.

Moreover, spending on administration depends significantly on customer choice. All private-sector alternatives are not equally costly. A variety of forms of insurance emerge, some very cheap, others not. For example, a 'catastrophe' insurance policy, which covers the individual against expensive emergencies but requires the policy-holder to meet, say, the first £500 of medical expenses in a year, is cheap. The same applies to HMOs. The subscriber pays a fixed amount, usually at monthly intervals, and receives all necessary care without further charge. The cost of administration is small. However, policies which offer comprehensive cover for every eventuality, including visits to the GP and/or spending on drugs, require the handling of a large number of small claims which raises costs. The insurer may have to calculate the patient's share, often 20 per cent, and this too costs time and money. Many continental national health insurance schemes, including the French system, are of this type.

It is not, therefore, possible to speak of 'the health insurance market' as if there were a single monolithic alternative. A major advantage of markets is that many ideas and alternative institutions can be tried out simultaneously. If a person wants 100 per cent cover for every expense, however small, the premiums will be high because many small pieces of paper have to be handled and many small cheques drawn. If, however, the patient pays all expenses up to a ceiling, the policy is cheaper to administer and requires lower premiums. Thus, consumers can choose between a range of insurance policies, some of which are cheap to administer and some not. If they choose to pay for costly policies, as they frequently do in America, that is their privilege, but the *average* cost of administering policies so chosen cannot properly be considered a flaw inherent in all health insurance schemes.

5

APPROACHES
TO REFORM

SIX MAIN approaches to the reform of the NHS can be identified: more money; efforts to increase efficiency; technocratic rationing; charges; national insurance; and private insurance. This chapter evaluates briefly the first five of these, whilst Chapter 6 considers how a private insurance market could be made to work.

1. More Money

In one view, there is nothing inherently wrong with tax finance, although there is short-run underfunding. The solution is to give the NHS more money and link the future allocation of finance to GDP or to guarantee a fixed percentage increase each year. The British Medical Association, for instance, recently called for an additional £1.5 billion to be injected into the NHS and for future funding to be adjusted upwards in accordance with increases in GDP. Such proposals would provide a temporary respite, but no more.

2. Increasing Efficiency

Others claim that the NHS has ample money but spends it inefficiently. In this view, therefore, the focus should be on improving efficiency, not on the size of the budget. This remains the principal stand taken by the Government.

The Government's health policy has three main aims:

(1) to increase spending in real terms, allowing for the growth in the number of elderly persons in the population as well as for the high cost of new technology;

(2) to bring about a regional equalisation of resources; and

(3) to promote cost saving by increasing efficiency.

Increased efficiency has been sought in three main ways: (a) by requiring health authorities to obtain tenders from the private sector for services like cleaning, laundry and catering; (b) by carrying out efficiency studies; and (c) by improving NHS management through the NHS management board and the introduction of general managers to run regional health authorities (RHAs), district health authorities (DHAs) and units within DHAs. The latter changes, characterised by the Government as a shift from an 'administered' to a 'managed' service, are regarded as pivotal. According to the Minister for Health, Mr Tony Newton:

> 'The health service is going through a period of major reshaping. It is being changed from being an administered service to being a managed service. That is very important, and more significant than most people have yet appreciated'.[1]

As a further step in the same direction, the idea of an 'internal market' in NHS services was advocated by Professor Alain Enthoven in 1985.[2] His chief objective was to remove the obstacles to patient movements across DHA boundaries. At present the rules governing the re-imbursement of health authorities which treat patients from other DHAs discourage them from treating outsiders. They receive the average cost for the particular procedure and not their actual expenditure, and in any event are paid two budget cycles later. For this reason, some DHAs have a policy of not admitting patients from outside their own area.

Although cross-boundary flows are allowed for under the government's funding formula, if DHAs accepted patients on mutually acceptable terms instead of according to national guidelines, inter-authority co-operation in the treatment of patients could be much improved. Such an experiment is already beginning to develop in the London area, as long-established teaching hospitals like Guys and Barts struggle to maintain their present size by attracting new customers. Private sector facilities are also being used to reduce waiting lists in some areas.

A recent variation on the internal-market theme has been

---

[1] *British Medical Journal*, 7 February 1987, p. 383.
[2] Enthoven (1985).

proposed by the Adam Smith Institute.[1] In its view, the key to reform of the NHS lies in the re-organisation of its management structure. They propose that RHAs and DHAs should be replaced by Health Management Units (HMUs), modelled loosely on American HMOs. They would be funded from taxation and responsible for providing full care for patients registered with them through their general practitioner. The GP's decision to join an HMU would mean that his patients would follow. A patient dissatisfied with the HMU would leave by signing up with a GP registered with a different HMU. GPs would cease to be paid by a combination of capitation fees, basic salary and special allowances; instead they would be paid by the HMU according to work done. HMUs would not only pay GPs, they would also buy in services from hospitals, which would become independently managed units.

Given the radical image of the Adam Smith Institute, this scheme is surprisingly weak, and would not overcome the chief problems of the NHS. It does not enable people to determine how much to assign to health care and it does not overcome double payment, and thus allows continued obstruction of competition. Nor do consumers gain greater power of choice. A similar proposal, for the establishment of managed health care organisations (MHCOs), has been put forward by David Willetts and Dr Michael Goldsmith for the Centre for Policy Studies.[2] This proposal is rather more flexible and more consumer oriented than the Adam Smith Institute scheme, but also fails fully to confront the fundamental defects of the NHS.

To sum up: any improvement in the efficiency of the NHS is undoubtedly desirable, but not one of the proposals so far put forward overcomes the fundamental structural flaw in the NHS, namely, that there is no satisfactory link between budgetary assignment and demand.

3. Technocratic Rationing

Some economists argue that there is nothing wrong with tax finance as such, but that current rationing methods are too

---

[1] Butler and Pirie (1988a;1988b).
[2] Willetts and Goldsmith (1988).

arbitrary. Such critics contend that NHS rationing should be placed on a more technical footing by means of Quality Adjusted Life Years (QALYs). The weaknesses of this proposal have already been discussed in Chapter 1 (p.20).

4. NHS Charges

A fourth view is that the main burden can continue to be borne by taxation but that additional revenue should be raised from private sources through charges, commercial activities, or even a lottery. The chief weakness of proposals of this type is that relatively small sums of money are involved. There are stronger objections to NHS charges.

One of the main arguments being used in support of introducing a charge for GP consultations along the lines of the prescription charge is that frivolous visits to the doctor would be discouraged. Advocates of this measure believe that charges have something in common with market competition, but they appear to value pricing chiefly as a deterrent. Yet pricing is desirable only if people have alternatives available to them, so that the obligation to pay for services rendered is accompanied by the power to choose.

Fixed-rate charges for hospital accommodation would be as detrimental as GP charges. Some additional revenue would accrue to the Exchequer but hospitals would remain unresponsive to consumers, calling patients in *en bloc* instead of using an appointment system, or admitting patients for surgery only to send them home after a wait of an hour or two in reception, suitcase in hand, because of a shortage of beds. Above all, if hospital accommodation charges were enforced, people going into hospital would be paying more out of pocket for the NHS on top of the £1,500 a year already being paid in taxation by the average family, and they would still have no guarantee of access to health-care services. The waiting lists would continue, and so would the denial of treatment.

5. National Insurance

Continued reliance on taxation to fund the NHS could be justified only if there were a 'correct' figure which could somehow be calculated by government. There is no such figure, and even if there were, a government would always have to take into account other considerations such as the strength of the economy and demands from other government departments. As the pace of change in medical technology quickens and increasing prosperity brings rising public demands, so governments will find the obligation to finance the NHS from taxation a growing source of political dissatisfaction.

In a recent paper published by the Conservative Political Centre, Leon Brittan, MP, has advocated the introduction of national health insurance.[1] He envisages that all spending on the NHS should come from a new National Health Insurance Scheme. National insurance contributions in their present form would be abolished and the national insurance benefits funded from general taxation. They would be replaced by National Health Insurance contributions which would be set at a level to meet the cost of the NHS, less income from charges. The total contribution would be met by the individual and there would, apparently, be no employer contribution. The attraction of the proposal, according to Mr Brittan, is that when individuals contemplated whether or not to call for more spending on the NHS they would be aware of the full impact of an increase or decrease on their own family budget.

To encourage, or at least avoid discouraging, people from spending on private insurance they would be free to opt out of part or all of the National Health Insurance Scheme. Brittan envisages that people might, for instance, be able to opt out of all NHS health-care services except GP or emergency treatment. Individuals opting out would have to take out private insurance to a standard considered satisfactory by a new regulatory agency. According to Mr Brittan, the scheme would retain the 'rightly sacrosanct' principle behind the creation of the NHS, treatment for all irrespective of means. It would also promote competition and therefore help to raise standards for all. And it would not mean that the poor were locked into a second-class service.

Leon Brittan's scheme has much to commend it and certainly would be an improvement on the NHS, but it also has

---

[1] Brittan (1988).

some drawbacks. A particular disadvantage is that reform of the funding of the NHS has been linked to a reform in the method of funding all the present national insurance benefits. This makes the exercise more complex than it need be and introduces additional problems into an area already complex enough. There are also some question-marks against national insurance as such.

National insurance might work if total health-care spending was financed wholly from national insurance contributions. If it were, and if the contributions were separately identified on pay slips, and personal payments varied according to the choice of insurance policy individuals had made, then the national insurance contribution would be more like a price than a tax. In practice, however, overseas governments with national insurance schemes have rarely had the discipline to confine health spending to income raised from national insurance contributions. Most foreign national insurance schemes are systems of earmarked taxation, with further funds coming from general taxation. Because the national insurance basis of payment gives people rights to treatment, governments have experienced great difficulty in controlling their spending. Detailed reactions have varied from country to country, but have usually involved a combination of cost-sharing with patients and direct government price regulation, entailing detailed control of doctors' fees, hospital re-imbursement rates, hospital construction and new equipment purchases. These efforts to control prices and capital expenditure have invariably achieved little and often had perverse effects, as we have seen in Germany, where the price-fixing machinery has fallen under the sway of the organised medical profession. The promotion of price competition under national insurance schemes has rarely been attempted. Thus, we can gain some insights from the study of national insurance schemes, but we can learn little about the potential for price competition, which is largely absent.

The concrete experience of countries with national insurance, therefore, is not encouraging. They do not have the underfunding problem of the NHS, but instead they have an overfunding problem.

Radical but Evolutionary Change Necessary

I have argued that the NHS suffers from severe structural flaws and that radical change is, therefore, necessary, but this presents an immediate dilemma. One of the merits of a market is that events can unfold gradually as lessons are learnt from the trial and error of the competitive process. There has been a tendency in the past for governments to try to discover the 'correct' or 'optimal' system or structure for the supply of health care; having discovered it, to declare an Appointed Day; and to deem that from that day the new structure applies. But this approach is inconsistent with the evolutionary spirit of the market. This means that there can be no escape from the NHS in one fell swoop. Instead, we must search for a way in which we can remove obstacles to change and allow the wide experimentation which makes it more likely that good ideas will flourish and bad ones do the minimum of harm.

I have not, therefore, sought to discover the 'correct' or 'optimal' *structure* for the supply of health-care services, but rather to understand the *process* which will enable medical services in Britain to evolve in response to economic and social realities and personal and family choice. The role of government, according to this approach, is not to seek some new organisational framework — such as health management units or managed health care organisations — as if that would provide the ultimate remedy, but rather to try to identify the legal and political framework within which health-care services can grow and develop in response to personal preferences.

The issues in health care are complex and there are no obvious right answers. For this reason, we should maximise the extent to which anyone who cares enough to make the effort is free to apply his or her ingenuity to solving problems, and to that end, we should seek to ensure the wide dispersal of resources and, therefore, of the power to attempt new solutions. This can be achieved only by switching from taxation to insurance. But can it be achieved in an evolutionary manner?

Private Insurance

The chief example of a private health insurance market is America, but the main difficulty is that the nature of the insurance industry there is significantly distorted by a huge and open-ended government tax subsidy to group health schemes. This tax subsidy is doubly disadvantageous. First, it puts people seeking to take out insurance as individuals rather than as group members at a substantial disadvantage, not least because the subsidy does not go to those financially most in need of it, such as individuals in low-paid jobs with no workplace health plan or people who lose their job. Second, it encourages a lack of cost-consciousness by individuals and employers. We cannot, therefore, look to America for an exact blueprint. It is not yet a fully competitive market, but if we are careful to disentangle the consequences of competition from the effects of clumsy government interference, we can deepen our understanding of how a private insurance market would work.

As I argue in Chapter 3, competition between insurers has led to the emergence of arrangements which cope well with the complex problems surrounding the funding and supply of health care. People can have more personal control over the range of services available to them than they can under the NHS. And, above all, if providers do not prove satisfactory, people can go elsewhere. There is an ever-present process of improvement and responsiveness, exemplified by the rise of HMOs and the competitive reactions to it. In the 1980s HMOs have been expanding fast. Some people, however, found the traditional HMO formula unsatisfactory, and this led to the emergence of PPOs offering discounted fees for using approved (preferred) doctors in combination with insurance cover for patients who wanted to turn to providers outside the approved panel. The competitive counter-reaction of HMOs has taken two forms. Individual practice associations, based on modified fee-for-service, have less restrictions than the traditional staff, group and network models, based on salary or capitation. And more recently still, 'open-ended' HMOs have developed combining the traditional approved panel with indemnity insurance for non-panel doctors, allowing people to benefit from HMO cost-containment without such severe limitations on their choice.

This sort of responsiveness occurs only because people can switch their money into organisations which suit their

69

requirements better. Without the power to make such choices, consumers will always be in a weak position. To date, private insurance has proved the most promising way of putting consumers in the driving seat.

6

GETTING FROM
A TO B

How COULD Britain move to an insurance-funded system? The difficulty is that we cannot get to a situation in which everyone who is capable of independent choice pays their own way in one move. Some intermediate steps are necessary. The underlying principle I will follow is that the NHS should continue to rely on taxation, but that people who are dissatisfied should not be forced to pay for the NHS if they are not happy with the service they are receiving. No system will ever be responsive to consumers if producers receive payment whether or not their work is satisfactory. It follows that if consumers are dissatisfied they must be free to go to an alternative and to retrieve all or part of the taxes they have already paid.[1]

At present about 5 million people have private health insurance. This number would probably be considerably larger if people had not already been forced to pay for the NHS through taxes. The freedom to opt for cover by an alternative insurer and to take all or part of their tax payment with them would give an equal opportunity for everyone to become a private patient, whether rich or poor.

The freedom to go private is very popular, as a series of surveys carried out by my colleagues Ralph Harris and Arthur Seldon in 1963, 1965, 1970, 1978 and 1987 has repeatedly shown.[2] Ordinary opinion polls are no less convincing. According to an NOP poll published in February 1987, for instance, 75 per cent of respondents *dis*agreed when asked whether they

---

[1] This is a development of an idea first proposed in D.G. Green, 'Awakening Market Suppressed by the NHS', *Economic Affairs*, February-March 1986, pp. 28-9; and further developed in a paper presented to the PPP Company Conference on 9 November 1987.
[2] Harris and Seldon (1987).

thought that all private medicine should be abolished. Similarly, 71 per cent *dis*agreed with the statement that 'no doctor should be allowed to see private patients'. This and similar surveys conducted over many years show that the vast majority of people, regardless of their party political affiliation, have no objection to private medicine. Indeed they like to feel that they can personally go private if they so desire.

Granting individuals a right to opt out also has the merit of not forcing change on anyone who does not want it. There will be some people who want to remain covered by the NHS and in any event it is a huge organisation, difficult to reform. Moreover, staff currently employed by the NHS will undoubtedly resist change and this scheme makes allowance for their legitimate fears. Anxiety in the face of impending change is understandable, but no one has the right to demand that alternatives be suppressed. Any citizen, however, does have the right to ask to be given a fair chance to compete, and this scheme gives NHS staff just such an opportunity.

If this approach is followed, two particular issues will require immediate resolution. First, should the poor be treated as a residual group, or incorporated into the insurance system, and if so on what terms? Second, what should happen to the NHS? Should it remain essentially intact, whilst allowing people to opt out if they so choose; or will some additional internal reform be necessary?

I will argue that people unable to afford insurance should be incorporated into the insurance system. Australia for many years issued a health card giving the holder free access to public hospitals, a system which worked well for a long period without it being suggested that the poor were receiving an inferior service. However, I will argue that the poor should also enjoy a measure of market power. This will require the government to give the poor sufficient money to buy access to that set of health-care services believed to be essential, a matter to which I return below (p.81).

But what would happen to the NHS? In addition to allowing people the freedom to opt out, there is also much to gain from reforming the NHS, so that as private alternatives emerge the NHS general managers are able to compete without having their hands tied behind their backs. Proposals for re-structuring the NHS would be best introduced as pilot schemes in one or more regions, again to facilitate evolutionary rather than sudden change.

Some key matters are controlled regionally or nationally, thus stifling the scope of local managers. Wages, for instance, are agreed in national negotiations, thereby denying local management a vital means of motivating their staff to perform better. If district health authorities became autonomous, receiving their budgets directly from the Treasury, and with responsibility for both revenue and capital budgets, some of these rigidities could be mitigated. The regional health authorities would be left with little to do and could be disbanded.

It would also be desirable to wind up the DHAs as such, and to make the district general managers responsible for the provision of services. At present, authorities tend to be dominated by producer interests, and this hampers the ability of general managers to become more responsive to consumers. DHAs must comprise a minimum of 16 members. The chairman is appointed by the Secretary of State. Members must include one hospital consultant, one general practitioner, one nurse/midwife/health visitor, one nominee from the Region's medical school, one trade union member, four (or more) local authority nominees and seven (or more) general members appointed by the Region. Instead of responsibility resting with these 16-member committees, general managers should be given full control. They would be appointed by and accountable to the NHS Management Board.

Reform of the consultants' contracts would also be desirable. At present many general managers feel they do not have the loyalty of their consultants, the key staff in meeting consumer demand, because (in non-teaching districts) their contracts are held at regional level. This could be overcome if consultants were employed by districts on fixed-term contracts of around five years.

To help encourage a sense of common purpose amongst staff and to facilitate without actually promoting greater private hospital ownership, it could also be made possible for the general manager and staff of an NHS hospital or district to buy out the service they manage. Such a management buy-out option would give the staff of NHS hospitals an opportunity to flourish in competition with private hospitals, so long as they are able to raise their standards sufficiently to be attractive to consumers. Beyond this I would make no immediate provision for privatisation, preferring to leave the fate of the public/private mix in hospital ownership to the personal choice of consumers of health care.

Personal Buying Power

I turn now to my main proposal which is built on two *already* popular principles: (a) that no one should go without essential health care due to an inability to pay; and (b) the right to go private. I envisage that people would have available to them two vouchers, one for hospital care and one for primary care, both weighted for age, to allow for the different demands made by different age groups. The figures presented below are for illustrative purpose only. The hospital voucher calculations are based on the actual expenditure per head in 1986 on the NHS hospital service, excluding long stay, adjusted for inflation. Long-stay provision for the elderly, mentally handicapped, mentally ill and physically disabled is excluded because these are 'caring' rather than 'curing' services which are best provided according to separate principles, as indeed the recent Griffiths report recognises.[1] The figures also exclude 'community' services, some of which are the proper object of government spending. The age weightings are based on those used by PPP for its insurance policies, weights which are not very different from BUPA's. Vouchers would be assigned as shown in Table 1.

How would different types of family fare under these arrangements? An elderly retired couple living alone would receive a voucher worth £550, a couple in the age group 45-54 with no children would get £244, and a couple aged 30-44 with two children under 18 would receive £300.

Primary-care vouchers are also based on spending in 1986, adjusted for inflation. In 1986 the average annual cost of Family Practitioner Services was £79 per head, of which £36 went on drugs and £26 on doctors' services. The remainder is accounted for by dentists and opticians. The primary-care

---

[1] Griffiths (1988).

Table 1

Hospital Vouchers

Age	Value of voucher per person, 1988 £
Under 18	48
18-29	88
30-44	102
45-54	122
55-64	174
65 plus	275

Table 2

Primary-Care Vouchers

Age	Value of voucher per person, 1988 £
Under 18*	21
18-29	17
30-44	19
45-54	24
55-64	33
65 plus	52

* Pre-teenage children make considerable use of primary services and it may be desirable to draw finer distinctions than those suggested here for illustrative purposes.

voucher covers the cost of GP services only, and excludes the cost of drugs. Again the figures would need to be weighted for age (Table 2).

How would individual families be affected? A retired couple with no children would receive £104, a couple with no children in the age group 45-54 would get £48, and a couple aged 30-44 with two children, £80.

The government should be neutral about the choice people make, offering special subsidies to neither the public nor private sectors. If people chose to take no action, they would receive care exactly as at present from the same GP and hospital. Regional health authorities would continue to be funded as at present and to parcel out funds to district health authorities, unless pilot schemes along the lines proposed above were established.

Or, people could take up the option of a hospital and/or a primary-care voucher. Two conditions would apply: they must relinquish their claim to free NHS services and take out private insurance to the value of the voucher or more. There is always a danger that people will under-estimate the risk of catastrophic illness and therefore under-insure. The expectation that government or private charity will pay for treatment may encourage this tendency still further, and for this reason it is permissible for government to require that all insurance policies should include coverage against catastrophic illness.

People who opted out could then turn either to private-sector or NHS hospitals for their treatment. They would not be confined only to using private hospitals. If they chose to use NHS services they would pay as private patients which would almost certainly mean an increase in the number of pay beds, preferably provided in separate buildings within the grounds of existing NHS hospitals. Individuals opting out of the NHS hospital service would continue to enjoy rights to long-stay care (for the mentally ill, mentally handicapped, physically disabled and geriatrics) and certain community services. There are no private hospitals providing emergency care at present and it would take time for them to develop such services. People opting out would therefore have no choice but to go to NHS hospitals for emergency treatment. In such cases bills would be presented to insurance companies. Given British traditions it is unlikely that this would lead to serious problems, but it may be advisable to put all hospitals under an obligation to 'stabilise' patients in emergencies before deciding where they should ultimately be treated. Standard prices for the stabilisation of emergency cases are likely to emerge. Anyone suffering an accident would have the absolute certainty of knowing that they would be treated.

For people choosing to contract out of the family doctor service alone there would be no obligation to take out insurance cover, because it is not an efficient way to pay for

GP services. But it is likely that insurers will emerge offering GP cover and particularly likely that HMOs, which integrate primary and secondary care, will develop. A family of four (with parents in the 30-44 age group) choosing a private HMO, for instance, would take with them £380 (a primary-care voucher of £80 and a hospital voucher of £300), a sum sufficient on its own to buy very good cover, even without topping up.

For those people who opt out, government will no longer face a commitment to finance an unlimited set of health-care services. Instead, government will make a fixed annual contribution based on spending in 1986 (which could be reviewed annually to avoid erosion by inflation) and people who want more services will be free to pay more. The pressures on the NHS will ease as individuals opt out, reducing the extent of the open-ended financial obligation faced by government. No one will be 'locked into' the NHS, because at any moment each person will be free to escape by choosing the voucher option. The payments could be made in more than one way. Probably the simplest would be to make an adjustment to tax codes, but this may come up against hostility from the Treasury, which currently favours simplifying the tax system. An alternative would be for government to make payments direct to the health purchase union (below, p.87) chosen by the individual or family.

The Regulatory Framework Necessary to Make Competition Work

In a competitive market in which insurers must compete for subscribers and doctors and hospitals for patients, then, as far as possible, any institution which human ingenuity can devise should be free to compete for buyers. The most urgent task is to fashion the legal framework which is undoubtedly necessary to direct the energies of a competitive insurance market into the service of all consumers. Four areas require particular attention: the tendency of provider groups to impede competition; the tendency of insurers to exclude high-risk individuals; the considerable advantages to be gained from buying insurance as a member of a pre-existing group; and the lack of purchasing power of the poor.

1. *Anti-Trust or Pro-Competition Laws*

The risk that the medical profession will subvert the competitive process is high. The organised medical profession should, therefore, be prevented from enforcing advertising bans, fixing prices, interfering with cost-containment efforts by insurers, impeding different types of delivery mechanism like HMOs, limiting the supply of doctors, and obstructing the emergence of competing professional or occupational groups. This will require the ending of government-sponsored professional self-regulation and changes in licensing laws. American experience of enforcing anti-trust law is set out in my study, *Challenge to the NHS*,[1] and some principles which might be applied to licensing reform in Britain are described in *Which Doctor?*.[2]

Governments should also be very careful in introducing reform not to play into the hands of the organised medical profession. When the 1911 National Insurance Act and the 1946 National Health Service Act were implemented, considerable co-operation was required from doctors and this was used to extract more money from taxpayer/patients and to re-inforce the power of organised medicine.

2. *Risk Selection*

When people take out insurance they each pay into a fund which they can draw on if a specified unwanted or costly event, such as illness, a motor accident or death, occurs. If the event insured against, such as falling ill, has already happened insurance companies do not normally offer insurance on the same terms as they would a fully fit person. In some cases they will charge a higher premium; in others they will exclude cover of the pre-existing condition for a specified period of, say, two years; in still others, they will refuse cover at all for the pre-existing condition, but insure the subscriber against any other ill-health; and in some cases they will refuse to insure a person at all. It is estimated that about 1 per cent of Americans are wholly unable to obtain health insurance.

It is understandable that insurance companies are reluctant

---

[1] Green (1986).
[2] Research Monograph 40, London: IEA, 1985.

to offer insurance to people who are already ill on the same terms as they would a healthy person. But insurers go a step further and also try to select people who are not only in good health but also least likely to fall ill. They do so to protect themselves against 'adverse selection'.

Adverse selection is the name given to the process whereby people assess their own risk status and buy insurance accordingly. Buyers of insurance may have better information than the insurer about the likelihood of their lodging a claim, and so an insurance company can find that it has inadvertently accepted a membership which claims at a higher rate than the average. Insurance companies try to overcome this problem by selecting low-risk subscribers, and particularly by excluding the elderly. One disadvantage of this tendency is that it reduces price competition, because, instead of promoting cost-effective health care, insurers try to select 'good lives'. In combination with the attractions of taking out insurance as a member of a group, the efforts of insurance companies to avoid adverse selection can put insurance cover beyond the reach of, not only the already sick, but also some fully fit people.

The reality of health insurance in America is that most people insure as a group, mainly based at the workplace. This is partly because the tax system encourages it, but also because there are economies of scale, that is, there are considerable advantages for insurers in taking subscribers in the form of a group of people formed for reasons unrelated to their health condition and who already have an established financial relationship with some central organisation, such as an employer, a professional association, or a bank or building society. This lowers the costs of collecting premiums and reduces the expense of checking up on everyone (underwriting).

Any given person seeking an insurance policy as an individual rather than as a group member, may be no less fit than the average group member, but in America the pool of people seeking health care as individuals contains a high proportion of unhealthy people. Insurance companies in the USA try to avoid these high-risk individuals by charging very high premiums for all individual policies. Healthy individuals, therefore, find themselves facing a prohibitively high premium because they have been lumped in with the pool of very bad individual risks.

Another way in which high-risk individuals are avoided and price competition reduced is market segmentation, that is, companies specialise in catering for a particular section of the population. For instance, companies may target their sales effort on the young and healthy not only by their advertising tactics but also by designing insurance plans likely to be of interest only to this group, such as insurance coverage with a very high deductible and significant co-insurance. There is a sense in which this strategy works to the disadvantage of others by 'creaming off' the most healthy people with the inevitable result that, other things being equal, average premiums for others must rise. Market segmentation also tends to reduce price competition. In the past, community rating has been advocated to eliminate such market segmentation, but community rating has the disadvantage that if insurance is voluntary then the healthiest people become disinclined to take out insurance at all, preferring to self-insure because they judge the cost of insurance to be excessive. Compulsory national insurance removes their freedom to self-insure, but it has other disadvantages, as we have seen.

Professor Enthoven, in his original *Consumer Choice Health Plan*,[1] urged that two rules would be necessary to prevent competition from producing such unwanted outcomes: (a) open enrolment, that is, a requirement that no one should be refused cover due to pre-existing ill-health; and (b) modified experience rating, that is, each insurer should charge subscribers in the same age group, e.g. the over-65s, the same premium. Premiums would differ from company to company but not for subscribers in the same age group covered by the same insurer. Enthoven believed that the two rules would encourage insurers to compete by seeking out cost-effective methods of health care instead of by becoming more adept at selecting 'good lives'. The rules would also mean that everyone would be incorporated into the health insurance system and so be able to enjoy personal buying power. The disadvantage of his 'modified experience rating' rule is that individual premiums cannot be adjusted to encourage a

---

[1] *Health Plan*, Reading, Mass.: Addison Wesley, 1980.

healthy lifestyle, for instance, by offering discounts to non-smokers. It could also have the perverse effect of discouraging competition, because, if applied nationally, an insurer would not be able to give discounts to group schemes, when rivalry for group business is one of the main forces making for price competition. There may, however, be a better way of preventing individual premiums from being excessively loaded, as I will consider below.

The open-enrolment rule, however, can be justified. The danger is that it might deter insurance companies from participation because many of those who will be attracted by the right to opt out of the NHS will be people on waiting lists who have already been diagnosed as sick. And there is no doubt that an open-enrolment rule is an infringement of pure insurance principles, for the obvious reason that the event being insured against has already happened. However, insurance companies have accommodated themselves to open-enrolment by means of occasional 'open seasons' in countries such as Australia and the USA, and there is no reason to suppose that insurers in Britain would be any different. It may be necessary, however, for government to make a special, one-off addition to the voucher to allow for the cost of treating pre-existing conditions. To be attractive to government, this adjustment would have to be less than the cost of treating the individual concerned under the NHS.

3. *Inclusion of the Poor*

One of the main arguments used against promoting personal choice is that a two-tier system will result. If the government funds health-care services for the poor but not for everyone then, so the argument runs, the poor will receive a poor quality service whilst people who can afford more will get superior care. Therefore, according to this line of reasoning, the government should finance health care for everyone and provide an equal service for them all. Some go so far as to advocate the abolition of the private sector to prevent the better-off buying extra services. The latter view has not carried much weight in recent years, largely because most people feel that if they want to go private they should be free to do so.

However, the idea that the government should finance

health care from taxation in order that everyone can obtain 'equal' service is still powerful. It has been the dominant philosophy for the last 40 years and, as I have argued, it has failed because, among other things, it is based on the mistaken view that all health care is like emergency care and that consequently it should be free. But more important still, despite the rhetoric about equality, everyone is not treated equally by the NHS. If you work in the NHS, or you are a VIP, or you 'know the ropes', then it will almost certainly be possible to gain privileged service for yourself. In getting good service from the NHS, 'middle-class know-how' is of more value than 'middle-class money'.

In a competitive market, however, the dissatisfied customer can go to another hospital, and this very freedom to go elsewhere makes it more likely that providers will take the trouble to please their customers. Moreover, the comparisons and rivalry, which are the essence of competition, make it more likely that the dissatisfied customer will produce a general supply response which benefits many others. Above all, the simple freedom to go to an alternative provider requires no special aptitudes and therefore aids those with few social skills as much as the articulate and educated. In the absence of competition, complaints by the ordinary citizen may be ignored or even punished.

To sum up: the NHS does not provide equal treatment for all. Nor could it. In practice it puts everyone in a weaker position than they would be if they were personally responsible for their own health care. The poor are supposed to enjoy the same rights of access to medical care as everyone else, but in the first place, access depends partly on social skills and the poor disproportionately lack these skills. And in the second, they have no enforceable *rights*, as the two recent court cases fought by the distraught parents of the Birmingham hole-in-the-heart babies revealed. If, however, the government delineated a package of health-care services which it considered to be the civilised minimum, put a price on this package, and gave the poor sufficient money in the form of a voucher to buy it, the poor would be better off. They would have a clear entitlement to a well-defined set of services which was bought-and-paid-for and enforceable at law.

Much depends, of course, on how comprehensive a set of services is to be covered under the government package. There is a continuing need for debate about the standard of care government should provide the poor and how it should be adjusted over time. Should it, for instance, try to define the package in terms of the seriousness of the patient's ill-health? Should waiting times be built in for non-urgent surgery? Should it be linked to the services which the NHS is supposed (but fails in practice) to provide? In the latter case, it would not include private rooms, private telephones, 'cordon-bleu' food and the generally higher amenities available in private hospitals; nor would it include cosmetic surgery or a right of access to experimental techniques until they were tried and tested, but otherwise it would make available all the usual clinical services.

There is a further danger that a future government will allow the value of the voucher to be eroded. This could be avoided, however, by linking its value to the actual average expenditure on health insurance of, say, the next 20 per cent of the population above the poverty line, thus allowing changes in demand to be reflected as well as changes flowing from rising (or falling) incomes. Such an arrangement would mean that, for the poor, governments were funding that element of medical care which I have suggested is a consumer good. But this cannot be escaped if the poor are to be given access to a satisfactory standard of care. The side-effects of financing all essential health care for a minority of the population, however, are nowhere near as severe as when government attempts to finance all health care for the whole population.

I make no final recommendation about the method of helping the poor because it can be achieved in more than one way. The important thing is for the government to be clear that it wants to give beneficiaries real buying power. There remains the problem of those who are just above the poverty line. If it is felt that additional help should be given, the best method would probably be to make an adjustment to family credit.

Would a voucher for the poor militate against cost-effectiveness? Holders of vouchers would be able to take their voucher to any one of several insurance carriers who would have to provide contracted services for the cost of the voucher.

Each insurance carrier would, therefore, have an incentive to make the money go as far as possible. There is, however, a danger of under-servicing. This is partly overcome by the legal obligation faced by the company, but it is not a perfect world and some vulnerable poor people would no doubt find themselves getting less than their entitlement, as they do now under the NHS. In America some HMOs overcome this by employing 'outreach' workers, a practice which would probably develop in Britain. Alternatively, voluntary organisations might take on this role. But above all, if this problem was explicitly acknowledged, instead of swept under the carpet by pretending that everyone is treated equally, as the NHS does, there would be more chance of reaching these vulnerable groups. But neither they, nor anyone else, is helped if everyone is denied the power to choose.

4. *Buying in Groups*

Membership of a group is advantageous to consumers, not only because it reduces the cost of administering their insurance policies, but also because it enables them to negotiate *en bloc* with several insurance companies, thus increasing their bargaining power. In addition, the most successful examples of competitive markets in health insurance are multiple-choice group schemes run by private and public sector employers including General Motors and the American Federal Government.[1] According to Professor Enthoven, the key to their success has been, not only that the group size enables a good price/quality package to be obtained from insurers, but also the ability of employers or 'sponsors' to control the design of the various insurance plans made available to employees and their active participation in framing the rules within which individuals make their choices.

This involvement in rule-making is essential to overcome the problems arising from adverse selection.[2] But it is not only the reactions of insurance companies to adverse selection that can be undesirable. Individual choice within multiple-choice schemes can also be abused. For instance, imagine a particular

---

[1] The American Federal Employees Health Benefits Plan is described in Chapter 2, p.35.
[2] Enthoven (1986), pp. 105-19.

family participating in a multiple-choice plan. For several years the family pays a low premium by choosing a policy with a high deductible. Then it learns that a family member needs an operation, but that the timing is not urgent. At the next open-enrolment period it switches to the HMO, paying a higher premium but entitling it to comprehensive care without further charge. The family member has the operation on the HMO, and then at the end of the year the family switches back to the cheaper high-deductible plan, anticipating that it will not need to claim very much in the forthcoming year.

The underlying problem is that the creative energy which leads companies to devise policies attractive only to the young and healthy, and the ingenuity individuals employ to get the best deal for their family, can have unwanted costs for everyone. But this very same creative force can be captured and channelled by competition for the benefit of all, and the practical problem is how to create the regulatory environment in which this can be achieved without the regulatory measures producing their own perverse effects. Measures to discourage excessive market segmentation and risk selection are desirable but it is very difficult to see how this can be achieved by government without it doing more harm than good.

A great many health economists have leapt from the discovery of problems ('market failures') in health-care markets to the assumption that government must take over. For instance, one of the arguments used in favour of the NHS is that it can act as a countervailing power to control professional fees, and the same argument is used to support the Canadian system of government finance through provincial re-imbursement agencies which set professional fees and hospital budgets. Canadian experience shows that governments can contain doctors' incomes by controlling fee schedules and setting global hospital budgets. But not without some countervailing costs. The essential element in Canadian success has been bargaining with the medical profession. Individual consumers cannot bargain, whereas groups can; and in Canada the provincial governments have performed this task. The question is: Does this bargaining need to take place at national or regional/provincial level by government, or can it be carried out in smaller groups than whole nations or provinces? Apart from producing a high level of conflict between medical employees and the government, including strikes, the chief disadvantage of the Canadian system is its inflexibility. For instance, fee-for-service re-imbursement has been set in concrete by government fixing of fee schedules, with the result that health maintenance organisations cannot develop in Canada as freely as they can over the frontier in America. And the focus on hospital budgets tends to discourage the provision of medical services in more cost-effective settings, such as local clinics and group practices.

The question I put is whether this inflexibility could be avoided if government did not take on the task of price-fixing but instead made it possible for voluntary associations of consumers or employer/sponsors to bargain with producers. According to Enthoven, this can be achieved.

It can be predicted that some individuals will be ingenious in seeking out opportunities to free ride and that insurance companies will use their ingenuity no less effectively to avoid high risks. According to Enthoven, this will require constant monitoring by employer/sponsors leading to regular revision of the rules governing the multiple-choice schemes and regular plan re-design to ensure fair play and to avoid unwanted or perverse outcomes.

The market power of employer/sponsors enables them to lay down the conditions on which they will make any given insurance policy available to employees, allowing them, for instance, to sift out plans oriented wholly towards 'cream skimming' the healthiest sections of the population. Because there is no single correct formula, and because there is merit in diversity, employer/sponsors can experiment with alternative ways of making multiple choices available to their employees without it leading to excessive market segmentation, ultimately at the expense of everyone. General Motors, for example, pays the whole insurance premium for its employees who then choose from a range of approved insurance plans, including over 140 HMOs, a PPO and two managed-care fee-for-service plans. In each case, General Motors has checked out the small print and laid down rules about coverage and to ensure fair play when individuals transfer from one plan to another. Insurance companies which do not toe the line lose access to a large market. Other companies with multiple-choice schemes exercise similar control over what insurers can offer, but each in their own way.

Thus, a competitive market in rule-making by 'sponsors' is required, allowing the detailed rules to be the subject of continuous bargaining between groups of buyers and insurers, so that trial and error throws up the best outcomes. It is not enough for governments to lay down a single framework, once and for all, though some general regulations will be necessary.

The validity of this important insight is supported, not only by contemporary American evidence, but also by British experience of providing health insurance before the NHS. Consumers in Britain joined mutual aid associations which negotiated a price/service package with individual doctors and framed rules governing the conduct of doctor and patient. Standards were upheld by competition and by an internal complaints machinery with the minimum of government involvement.[1] The development of these organisations was stifled by the monopolistic NHS.

Health Purchase Unions

But how could this bargaining power be incorporated into an opting-out scheme? For many people the 'natural' buying group will be their workplace, and it is possible that new consumer organisations may emerge spontaneously, but this will not guarantee that everyone is able to enjoy the advantages of group buying. Some American states have established 'risk pools' for people who cannot obtain health insurance. Based on this idea and on the pre-war experience of the British friendly societies, the British government should found one or more buyer groups which were open to anyone. Such buyer groups, called perhaps *health purchase unions*, would need to be independent of government. To that end they could be run by trustees who would employ managers on, say, a three-year franchise. The responsibility of the health purchase union would be to obtain the best deal for their members from insurers. As well as filtering out unsatisfactory insurance policies, health purchase unions could also self-insure and buy in some medical services direct.

[1] Green (1985).

Because it would take time to develop suitable expertise I would initially establish only four such health purchase unions, one each for England, Wales, Scotland and Northern Ireland, but provision should be made for additional ones to be founded in each region as it became realistic to expect to be able to recruit suitable staff and as the original national health purchase unions grew in size. Some general regulations would need to be applied, including an open-enrolment rule. The modified experience-rating rule, preventing the loading of individual insurance premiums, would be applied to all members of a health purchase union, but not to all subscribers of the same age covered by a particular company.

It would be too much of an infringement of freedom to prevent people from being individually insured if they wanted, but they would not be entitled to take their voucher direct to an insurance company. The voucher would be available only to people joining a health purchase union. This is coercive but justified by the technical difficulties of making a competitive market in health insurance work to the advantage of all.

Thus, health purchase unions comprise the final element in the opting-out scheme. People would take their optional voucher, not direct to an insurance company, but rather to a health purchase union, which would filter out unsatisfactory insurance plans and act as a consumer advocate, aiding individuals as they chose between this or that doctor or hospital. The government would initially found at least one statutory health purchase union in each of the four main parts of the United Kingdom to ensure that no one was left out and would authorise voluntary health purchase unions, which in the first instance would chiefly mean the recognition of employers as health purchase unions, though in due course other organisations would also be likely to fill the role.

Conclusion

The evidence from 40 years' experience of public *production* and *finance* through the NHS suggests that government should not attempt both to finance and produce health-care services. Instead, it should *finance* health care for those in need, to ensure that everyone has the power to buy health insurance cover, but it should not attempt to pay for all health-care services from taxation; it should *regulate*, by which I mean it should elaborate, refine, make and enforce the rules which enable a competitive market to serve the interests of all, rich and poor alike; and it should *publish* to enable people to make more effective choices.

Summary of Policy Proposals

o The NHS should be left intact, though pilot schemes to improve efficiency should be attempted.

o People dissatisfied with the NHS should be allowed to escape and to claim an age-weighted voucher representing the tax they had paid towards the NHS.

o They would be required to relinquish their claim to free NHS services and to take out private insurance to the value of the voucher or more, including catastrophe cover.

o Privately insured individuals or families could receive care, including emergency treatment, from the NHS as paying customers and would not be confined to using private hospitals.

o Separate vouchers would be available for hospital care (excluding long-stay) and primary care.

o The poor would receive a voucher sufficient to buy a specified set of health-care services.

o People opting out would take their voucher not direct to an insurance company but to a health purchase union, which would be responsible for making available several choices of insurance company.

o Most people will obtain cover through their employer or a private association, but in addition statutory health purchase unions independent of government would be established ultimately in each region (though initially only in each country of the UK).

o Insurance companies would be free to recruit individual subscribers, but they would not receive voucher payments unless the individual subscribed via a health purchase union.

REFERENCES

AMA (1985): *Socioeconomic Characteristics of Medical Practice*, Chicago: AMA.

AMCRA (1985): American Medical Care and Review Association, *Directory of Preferred Provider Organisations and the Industry Report on PPO Development*.

Arrow, K. (1963): 'Uncertainty and the welfare economics of medical care', *American Economic Review*, Vol. 53, pp. 941-73.

Bachman, S., Pomeranz, D. and Tell, E. (1987): 'Making employers smart buyers of health care', *Business and Health*, September, pp. 28-34.

Barr, N. (1987): *The Economics of the Welfare State*, London: Weidenfeld & Nicolson.

Boland, P. (1987): 'Trends in second-generation PPOs', *Health Affairs*, Winter, pp. 75-81.

Brittan, L. (1988): *A New Deal for Health Care*, London: Conservative Political Centre.

Buck, N., Devlin, H.B. and Lunn, J.N. (1987): *The Report of a Confidential Enquiry into Perioperative Deaths*, London: Kings Fund/Nuffield Provincial Hospitals Trust.

Butler, E. and Pirie, M. (1988a): *The Health of Nations*, London: Adam Smith Institute.

Butler, E. and Pirie, M. (1988b): *Health Management Units*, London: Adam Smith Institute.

Califano, J. (1986): *America's Health Care Revolution*, New York: Random House.

Charles, J.G. (1987): 'Using informed choice to combat health costs', *Business and Health*, September, pp. 36-8.

Chassin, M.R., *et al.* (1987): 'Does inappropriate use explain geographic variations in the use of health care services?', *Journal of the American Medical Association*. Vol. 258, No. 18, pp. 2,533-47.

Clare, F.L., Spratly, E., Schwab, P. and Iglehart, K. (1987): 'Trends in health personnel', *Health Affairs*, Winter, pp. 101-2.

Cochrane, A.L. (1972): *Effectiveness and Efficiency: Random Reflections on Health Services*, London: Nuffield Provincial Hospitals Trust.

Culyer, A.J. (1971): 'The nature of the commodity "health care" and its efficient allocation', *Oxford Economic Papers*, Vol. 23, pp. 189-211.

Culyer, A. and Posnett, J. (1985): 'Would you choose the welfare state?', *Economic Affairs*, Vol. 5, No. 2, pp. 40-42.

Enthoven, A. (1985): 'Health tax policy mismatch', *Health Affairs*, Vol. 4, No. 4, pp. 3-14.

Enthoven, A. (1985): *Reflections on the Management of the National Health Service*, London: Nuffield Provincial Hospitals Trust.

Enthoven, A. (1986): 'Managed competition in health care and the unfinished agenda', *Health Care Financing Review*, Annual Supplement, pp. 105-19.

Evans, R.G. (1984): *Strained Mercy: The Economics of Canadian Health Care*, Toronto: Butterworths.

Francis, W. (1985): *Checkbook's Guide to Health Insurance Plans for Federal Employees*, Washington: Checkbook.

Gabel, J. *et al.* (1987): 'The commercial health insurance industry in transition', *Health Affairs*, Fall, p. 47.

Goldberg, L.G. and Greenberg, W. (1977b): *The Health Maintenance Organisation and its Effects on Competition* (Federal Trade Commission Staff Report).

Gray, D., Marinker, M. and Maynard, A., 'The doctor, the patient, and their contract', *British Medical Journal*, 17 May 1986, pp. 1,313-5; 24 May 1986, pp. 1,374-6; 31 May 1986, pp. 1,438-40.

Green, D.G. (1985): *Working Class Patients and the Medical Establishment*, London: Gower.

Green, D.G. (1986): *Challenge to the NHS*, Hobart Paperback 23, London: IEA.

Green, D.G. (1987): *Medicines in the Marketplace*, London: IEA Health Unit.

Greenberg, W. (1984): 'Health care information in medical market-place reform', *Society and Health*, December, pp. 21-3.

Griffiths, Sir Roy (1988): *Community Care: Agenda for Action*, A report to the Secretary of State for Social Services by Sir Roy Griffiths, London: HMSO.

HHS (1986): *Statistical Outliers*. (A report of the Office of Medical Review, Health Standards and Quality Bureau, Health Care Financing Administration, HHS.)

Harris, R. and Seldon, A. (1987): *Welfare Without the State*, Hobart Paperback 26, London: IEA.

Interstudy (1986): *1986 June Update*, Excelsior, Minnesota: Interstudy.

Interstudy (1985a): *HMO Summary, June 1985*, Excelsior, Minnesota: Interstudy.

Interstudy (1985b): *National HMO Firms, 1985*, Excelsior, Minnesota: Interstudy.

Johns, L. and Jones, M.W. (1987): 'Physician response to selective contracting in California', *Health Affairs*, Winter, pp. 59-69.

Le Grand, J. (1988): 'Defending the NHS', *New Statesman*, 29 January, pp. 12,20.

Lewin and Associates (1984): *Synthesis of Private Sector Health Care Initiatives*. (A report prepared for the US Department of Health and Human Services.)

McKeown, T. (1979): *The Role of Medicine*, Oxford: Blackwell.

McLachlan, G. and Maynard, A. (eds.) (1982): *The Public/Private Mix for Health*, London: Nuffield Provincial Hospitals Trust.

McLachlan, G. and Maynard, A. (1982): 'The public/private mix in health care: the emerging lessons', in McLachlan and Maynard (1982), pp. 513-558.

91

McLaughlin, C.G. (1987): 'HMO growth and hospital expenses and use: a simultaneous-equation approach', *Health Services Research*. Vol. 22, No. 2, pp. 183-205.

Mill, J.S. (1970): *Principles of Political Economy* (1970 edn.), Harmondsworth: Penguin Books.

Mill, J.S. (1972): *On Liberty* (1972 edn.), London: Dent.

Neutra, R., *et al.* (1978): 'Effect of foetal heart monitoring on neonatal death rates', *New England Journal of Medicine*, Vol. 299, pp. 324-26.

OECD (1987): *Financing and Delivering Health Care*, Paris: OECD.

Robinson, J.C. and Luft, H.S. (1987): 'Competition and the cost of hospital care, 1972 to 1982', *Journal of the American Medical Association*, Vol. 257, No. 23, pp. 3,241-45.

Royal College of Surgeons (1986): *Commission on the Provision of Surgical Services*, London: RCS.

Schieber, G.J. and Poullier, J-P. (1987): 'Recent trends in international health care spending', *Health Affairs*, Fall, pp. 105-12.

Ware, J., *et al.* (1986): 'Comparison of health outcomes at a health maintenance organisation with those of fee-for-service care', *The Lancet*, 3 May, pp. 1,017-22.

Whitney, R, (1988): *National Health Crisis: A Modern Solution*, London: Shepheard-Walwyn.

Willetts, D. and Goldsmith, M. (1988): *Managed Health Care: a New System for a Better Health Service*, London: Centre for Policy Studies.

Yelin, E.H., *et al.* (1985): 'A comparison of the treatment of rheumatoid arthritis in health maintenance organisations and fee-for-service practices', *New England Journal of Medicine*, 11 April, pp. 962-67.

Everyone a Private Patient

The NHS is in crisis. It suffers from rising expectations, poor management and endemic under-funding. These problems are accepted by all sides to the debate. What is not agreed is the diagnosis of the causes and the solutions.

Everyone a Private Patient presents a refreshing analysis of the NHS which goes back to fundamentals. It challenges those who argue that more public money and better management will be sufficient to remedy its chronic deficiencies. Based on the precepts of patient choice and diversity in the supply of health care, Dr David Green argues that without a radical and innovative reform the NHS as presently organised will always be confronted by most of its present problems. Dr Green presents a comprehensive study of health financing. He offers analysis and evidence of the superiority of private insurance arrangements as a means of funding health care. *Everyone a Private Patient* examines the theory, evidence and proposals in detail. It concludes that health care is much too complex to admit of a single or simple solution. Its practical proposals are offered as a constructive contribution to a long-overdue public debate.

Summary of Contents

ISBN 0-255 36210-2

Hobart Paperback 27 is published by

£7·50

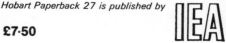

The Institute of Economic Affairs
2 Lord North Street, Westminster
London SW1P 3LB
Telephone: 01-799 3745

IEA PUBLICATIONS
Subscription Service

An annual subscription is the most convenient way to obtain our publications. Every title we produce in all our regular series will be sent to you immediately on publication and without further charge, representing a substantial saving.

Individual subscription rates*

Britain: £25·00 p.a. including postage.
£23·00 p.a. if paid by Banker's Order.
£15·00 p.a. to teachers and students who pay *personally*.

Europe: £25·00 p.a. including postage.

South America: £35·00 p.a. or equivalent.

Other Countries: Rates on application. In most countries subscriptions are handled by local agents. Addresses are available from the IEA.

* These rates are *not* available to companies or to institutions.

To: The Treasurer, Institute of Economic Affairs,
2 Lord North Street, Westminster,
London SW1P 3LB

I should like to subscribe from ....

I enclose a cheque/postal order for:

☐ £25·00

☐ £15·00   I am a teacher/student at ....

....

☐ Please send a Banker's Order form.

☐ Please send an invoice.

☐ Please charge my credit card:

Please tick   ☐ VISA ☐ ◣ ☐ AMERICAN EXPRESS ☐ ◍

Card No: ☐☐☐☐☐☐☐☐☐☐☐☐☐☐☐☐☐☐

In addition I would like to purchase the following previously published titles: *BLOCK LETTERS PLEASE*

....

....

Name   ....

Address ....

....

.... Post Code ....

Signed .... Date ....

Recent IEA Papers on Health Care, the NHS, Education and the Welfare State

Hobart Paperback 23
Challenge to the NHS
A study of competition in American health care and the lessons for Britain
David G. Green
1986   xx + 116pp   £4·00

'Professional monopolies have lasted longer than individual monopolies but in the United States the era of their security has now passed, as ... this provocative report from the Institute of Economic Affairs lucidly describes.'
British Medical Journal

Research Monograph 40
Which Doctor?
A critical analysis of the professional barriers to competition in health care
David G. Green
1985   £2·50

'A powerful attack is published today on the way the monopoly power of the British medical profession blocks all improvements that could benefit National Health Service patients.'   *Financial Times*

'... a lively, informative and in parts, original polemic which deserves a wide readership.'   *Economic Journal*

'If the track record of the Institute of Economic Affairs is anything to go by Green's tract may be a signal that these issues need to be tackled if some of the wilder ideas are not to take political root.'   Rudolf Klein,
British Medical Journal

Research Monograph 39
Competition and Home Medicines
W. Duncan Reekie and **Hans G. Ötzbrugger**
1985   £1·80

'It deserves a read, and – so far as I am aware – the OFT has left the retail chemists well alone hitherto. From what Messrs Reekie and Ötzbrugger have to tell us, this is perhaps an omission.

'Put simply, their thesis is that, if Norman Fowler wants to save some more money for the NHS ... then, instead of stamping on the fingers of the drugs firms, he could try loosening up on self-prescribing ...'
Jock Bruce-Gardyne, *Sunday Telegraph*

Hobart Paperback 21
The Riddle of the Voucher
An inquiry into the obstacles to introducing choice and competition in state schools
Arthur Seldon
1986   xii + 100pp   £3·50

'As a guide through this exciting but heavily mined country I can do no better than recommend [this] new pamphlet ...'
Ferdinand Mount, *The Spectator*

SOCIAL SCIENCE LIBRARY

Manor Road Building
Manor Road
Oxford OX1 3UQ
Tel: (2)71093 (enquiries and renewals)
http://www.ssl.ox.ac.uk

This is a NORMAL LOAN item.

We will email you a reminder before this item is due.

Please see http://www.ssl.ox.ac.uk/lending.html
for details on:

- loan policies; these are also displayed on the notice boards and in our library guide.

- how to check when your books are due back.

- how to renew your books, including information on the maximum number of renewals. Items may be renewed if not reserved by another reader. Items must be renewed before the library closes on the due date.

- level of fines; fines are charged on overdue books.

Please note that this item may be recalled during Term.

WITHDRAWN

Occ

The
For
Dav
198:
'The
for
bene
for t
'The
and
clair
'D
beca

IEA
Pape

Med
A st
pres
Dav
1987
'If Da
is an
Dr G
argu
good
'Dr C
and
rathe

Pape

Effi
A C
Ray
1988

Pape

Acc
Essa
Rudon Klein · Robert Pinker · Peter Collison · A. J. Culyer
Edited by **David G. Green**
1988   viii + 64pp   £8·95

302560578